MULTIPLE SCLEROSIS COOKBOOK

MEGA BUNDLE – 4 Manuscripts in 1 – 160+ Multiple Sclerosis - friendly recipes including casseroles, stew, side dishes, and pasta for a delicious and tasty diet

TABLE OF CONTENTS

advice is necessary, legal or professional, a practiced individual in the profession should be ordered.

- From a Declaration of Principles which was accepted and approved equally by a Committee of the American Bar Association and a Committee of Publishers and Associations.

Introduction

Multiple Sclerosis recipes for personal enjoyment but also for family enjoyment. You will love them for sure for how easy it is to prepare them.

ROAST RECIPES

ROASTED BEET

Serves: **3-4**

Prep Time: **10** Minutes

Cook Time: **20** Minutes

Total Time: **30** Minutes

INGREDIENTS

- 2 lb. beet
- 2 tablespoons olive oil
- 1 tsp curry powder
- 1 tsp salt

DIRECTIONS

1. Preheat the oven to 400 F
2. Cut everything in half lengthwise
3. Toss everything with olive oil and place onto a prepared baking sheet
4. Roast for 18-20 minutes at 400 F or until golden brown
5. When ready remove from the oven and serve

ROASTED RADISH

Serves: **3-4**

Prep Time: **10** Minutes

Cook Time: **20** Minutes

Total Time: **30** Minutes

INGREDIENTS

- 2 lb. radish
- 2 tablespoons olive oil
- 1 tsp curry powder
- 1 tsp salt

DIRECTIONS

1. Preheat the oven to 400 F
2. Cut everything in half lengthwise
3. Toss everything with olive oil and place onto a prepared baking sheet
4. Roast for 18-20 minutes at 400 F or until golden brown
5. When ready remove from the oven and serve

ROASTED SQUASH

Serves: 2

Prep Time: *10*   Minutes

Cook Time: 25   Minutes

Total Time: *35*   Minutes

INGREDIENTS

- 2 tablespoons olive oil
- salt
- 3 delicata squash

DIRECTIONS

1. Preheat oven to 400 F
2. Clean the delicate squash and cut in halft lengthwise
3. Scoop out the seeds and cut each half into 1/2 inch pieces
4. Place them on a baking pan and coat with olive oil
5. Bake for 12-15 minutes remove and place into a pan
6. Cook for 8-10 minutes remove, add salt, and serve

ZUCCHINI SOUP

Serves: **4**

Prep Time: **10**   Minutes

Cook Time: **20**   Minutes

Total Time: **30**   Minutes

INGREDIENTS

- 1 tablespoon olive oil
- 1 lb. zucchini
- ¼ red onion
- ½ cup all-purpose flour
- ¼ tsp salt
- ¼ tsp pepper
- 1 can vegetable broth
- 1 cup heavy cream

DIRECTIONS

1. In a saucepan heat olive oil and sauté zucchini until tender
2. Add remaining ingredients to the saucepan and bring to a boil
3. When all the vegetables are tender transfer to a blender and blend until smooth
4. Pour soup into bowls, garnish with parsley and serve

BLACK-EYE PEA FRITTERS

Serves: **2**

Prep Time: **10**   Minutes

Cook Time: **20**   Minutes

Total Time: **30**   Minutes

INGREDIENTS

- 1 cup dry black-eye peas
- 6 tablespoons water
- coconut oil
- 1 tsp apple cider vinegar
- ½ cup onion
- ¼ tsp cayenne pepper
- ½ tsp salt

SAUCE

- 1 cup onions
- salt
- 2 tablespoons coconut oil
- 1 cup red pepper
- ½ cup tomatoes
- ¼ tsp cayenne pepper

DIRECTIONS

1. For the sauce puree tomato, red pepper, pepper and add oil
2. Cook the puree until the liquid is evaporated for 10 minutes and set aside
3. In a food processor add cayenne pepper, black-eye peas, onions over medium speed, add water if necessary
4. Fry black eye pea fritters into oil, drop them into oil and let them fry for 2-3 minutes or until crispy, serve with sauce

PEAS WITH ONION CREAM SAUCE

Serves: *3*

Prep Time: *10*   Minutes

Cook Time: *20*   Minutes

Total Time: *30*   Minutes

INGREDIENTS

- 1 onion
- ½ tsp salt
- 2 oz. Swiss cheese
- 1 tablespoon butter
- ½ cup milk
- 1 cup water
- 6 oz. green peas
- 6 hard-boiled eggs
- ½ cup heavy cream
- ½ tsp black pepper

DIRECTIONS

1. In a saucepan add onion, water and boil for 4-5 minutes
2. Place the peas in a casserole and add hard-boiled eggs over them
3. Place the onion in blender and blend until smooth,
4. In a saucepan melt butter and add cornstarch, add milk and bring to boil

5. Add cream, onion puree, salt and pepper
6. Pour mixture over sliced eggs and sprinkle with Swiss cheese
7. Serve when ready

Serves: **4**
Prep Time: **10**   Minutes

Cook Time: **30**   Minutes

Total Time: **40**   Minutes

INGREDIENTS

- 2 cups cooked pigeon peas
- 1 cup white rice
- 1 tsp dried thyme
- 1 can coconut milk
- 1 habanero pepper
- 1 cup water
- 2 cloves garlic
- salt

DIRECTIONS

1. Place all ingredients in a saucepan and bring to boil
2. Simmer until liquid is absorbed, simmer for 20-30 minutes
3. Remove the habanero and serve

Serves: **4**

Prep Time: **10**   Minutes

Cook Time: **30**   Minutes

Total Time: **40**   Minutes

INGREDIENTS

- 3 cups kohlrabi
- 6 cups vegetable broth
- 2 tablespoons olive oil
- ½ cup onion
- 1 cup white rice
- 1 garlic clove
- salt
- 1 cup white wine
- 1 tsp white pepper
- ½ cup Parmesan cheese
- ½ tsp nutmeg
- 1 tsp butter

DIRECTIONS

1. In a saucepan add vegetable stock and bring to a simmer

2. In another saucepan heat olive oil, add onion, garlic and cook until tender, add diced kohlrabi and cook for 5-10 minutes or until tender

3. Add rice and stir the grains, add wine and stir until evaporated

4. Add stock over the rice to cover it, add a couple of ladlefuls and continue to cook

5. When the rice is tender add pepper and salt

6. Stir in parmesan cheese and serve

Serves: **2**

Prep Time: **5**   Minutes

Cook Time: **15**   Minutes

Total Time: **20**   Minutes

INGREDIENTS

- 4 oz. spaghetti
- 2 cups basil leaves
- 2 garlic cloves
- ¼ cup olive oil
- 2 tablespoons parmesan cheese
- ½ tsp black pepper

DIRECTIONS

1. Bring water to a boil and add pasta
2. In a blend add parmesan cheese, basil leaves, garlic and blend
3. Add olive oil, pepper and blend again
4. Pour pesto onto pasta and serve when ready

CILANTRO SLAW

Serves:	**2**
Prep Time:	**5** Minutes
Cook Time:	**5** Minutes
Total Time:	**10** Minutes

INGREDIENTS

- 2 cups chopped cabbage
- 1 cup romaine lettuce
- ½ cup cilantro
- 1 tablespoon lime juice
- 1 tablespoon olive oil

DIRECTIONS

1. In a bowl mix cilantro, cabbage and lettuce
2. In another bowl mix olive oil and lime juice
3. Pour dressing over mixture and toss to coat and serve

LIME RICE

Serves: **4**

Prep Time: **10**   Minutes

Cook Time: **30**   Minutes

Total Time: **40**   Minutes

INGREDIENTS

- 1 cup rice
- 1 tablespoon olive oil
- 2 tablespoons lime juice
- 1 cup water
- ¼ tsp salt
- ½ cup cilantro

DIRECTIONS

1. In a bowl add water, rice, salt and bring to boil
2. Simmer for 20 minute or until water is absorbed
3. In a bowl mix olive oil, cilantro and lime juice
4. Add rice to the mixture and serve

FRIED APPLES

Serves: **6**
Prep Time: **10** Minutes

Cook Time: **10** Minutes

Total Time: **20** Minutes

INGREDIENTS

- 6 apples
- 2 tablespoons butter
- ½ tsp cinnamon
- honey

DIRECTIONS

1. **In a saucepan melt butter and add slices of apple, sauté until tender**
2. **Sprinkle the cinnamon and honey**
3. **Stir to coat and serve**

LOW OXALATE BURGERS

Serves: **4**
Prep Time: **10**   Minutes

Cook Time: **30**   Minutes

Total Time: **40**   Minutes

INGREDIENTS

- 1 tablespoon lemon juice
- ¼ tsp ginger
- ¼ lb. beef
- salt
- 2 tablespoons Sunbutter

DIRECTIONS

1. In a skillet add lemon juice, ginger and cook for a couple of minutes
2. Shape the beef into patties and grill in a skillet over medium heat
3. Melt the Sunbutter until smooth and add melted Sunbutter on each patty
4. Serve with gluten-free sandwich bread

CAULIFLOWER MASHED POTATOES

Serves: **4**

Prep Time: **10**   Minutes

Cook Time: **25**   Minutes

Total Time: **35**   Minutes

INGREDIENTS

- 2 lbs. white potatoes
- 1 head cauliflower
- ½ cup goat cheese
- ½ cup olive oil
- salt

DIRECTIONS

1. Steam the cauliflower and potatoes for 20 minutes or until soft
2. In a food processor add cauliflower and mashed potatoes
3. Add olive oil, goat cheese and puree until smooth
4. Mash the potatoes and add in the cauliflower cheese mixture
5. Season with salt, pepper and and serve

HAMBURGER WITH MUSHROOMS

Serves: *8*
Prep Time: *10*   Minutes

Cook Time: *30*   Minutes

Total Time: *40*   Minutes

INGREDIENTS

- 1.5 lbs. ground chuck
- 1 egg
- ½ cup red onion
- 1 tsp garlic powder
- salt
- 10 stuff mushrooms
- 1 tsp garlic powder

DIRECTIONS

1. In a bowl mix all ingredients, form small patties
2. In a pan heat oil over medium heat and add the patties
3. Cook on both sides until dark caramelized
4. Bake mushrooms at 375 F until tender, remove and serve with hamburgers

CABBAGE BEEF WRAPS

Serves: **4**

Prep Time: **10**   Minutes

Cook Time: **20**   Minutes

Total Time: **30**   Minutes

INGREDIENTS

- 1 head of cabbage
- ½ head of cauliflower
- ¼ cup cremeni mushrooms
- ¼ cup green onions
- ¼ tsp ginger
- ¼ tsp garlic
- 1 tablespoon vegetable oil
- 1 lb. beef

STIRFRY SAUCE

- 1 cup shiikate mushrooms
- ¼ cup green onions
- 1 tsp ginger
- 1 tsp garlic
- ¼ piece bacon sliced
- 2 drops sesame oil
- 1 tablespoon ketchup
- ½ cup wine vinegar

- ¼ cup water
- 1 tablespoon butter
- 1 tablespoon vegetable oil
- sriracha

DIRECTIONS

1. For Stir fry sauce add onions, ginger, garlic, mushrooms and bacon into a pan, add oil and cook on medium heat for 10-12 minutes

2. Puree the ingredients and add sesame oil, salt, water, ketchup and pepper, blend until smooth

3. Remove and add sriracha to the sauce

4. For rolls toss the cabbage in vegetable oil, salt and lay on a baking sheet

5. Bake for 10-12 minutes at 325 F

6. In a wok add vegetable oil, add the beef, vegetables, ginger, garlic and sauce well

7. Add sauce and serve in the cabbage cups and top with onions

GINGER PUMPKIN CUSTARD

Serves: **6**

Prep Time: **10**   Minutes

Cook Time: **50**   Minutes

Total Time: **60**   Minutes

INGREDIENTS

- 2 cups pumpkin puree
- 1 tablespoon raw ginger
- 1 tsp nutmeg
- 1 tsp vanilla extract
- 2 eggs
- ¾ cup cream
- ½ cup honey

DIRECTIONS

1. Preheat oven to 300 F
2. In a bowl mix all ingredients and stir until well mixed
3. Place mixture into a baking dish and bake for 45 minutes
4. Remove and serve

ROASTED BRUSSEL SPROUTS

Serves: *4*

Prep Time: *10*   Minutes

Cook Time: *30*   Minutes

Total Time: *40*   Minutes

INGREDIENTS

- 1.2 lbs. Brussel sprouts
- 1 tsp grated ginger
- 1 tablespoon maple syrup
- 1 tablespoon olive oil
- 1 tablespoon butter
- salt

DIRECTIONS

1. Heat up oven to the broil
2. Toss the Brussel sprouts with the ginger, salt and olive oil
3. Spread on a baking sheet and bake for 4-5 minutes
4. Remove, add maple syrup, mix well and bake for another 3-4 minutes
5. Remove and serve

Serves: **4**

Prep Time: **10**   Minutes

Cook Time: **30**   Minutes

Total Time: **40**   Minutes

INGREDIENTS

- 1 head cauliflower
- 1 clove garlic
- 1 tablespoon butter
- 1 tablespoon olive oil
- ¼ green onions
- 1 tablespoon parmesan cheese
- salt
- 2 potatoes
- 1 cup goat cheese
- ½ yellow onion

DIRECTIONS

1. In a pot add water, potatoes and cauliflower
2. Add in a stainless-steel steam basket to the pot, add cauliflower and potatoes
3. Cook for 18-20 minutes

4. Sauté the onions and garlic with olive oil and butter, cook until golden brown

5. Add goat cheese, onion mixture, potatoes and cauliflower in a food processor and pulse until smooth

6. Add in the green onions and pulse again

7. Place mixture into a casserole dish and top with parmesan cheese

8. Broil for a couple of minutes and serve

QUINOA FALAFEL

Serves: **6-8**

Prep Time: **15** Minutes

Cook Time: **25** Minutes

Total Time: **40** Minutes

INGREDIENTS

- 2 cups cooked quinoa
- 2 cups chickpeas
- 1 onion
- 1 tablespoon tahini
- 4 garlic cloves
- 1 cup parsley
- 2 tsp cumin
- 1 tsp coriander
- 2 tablespoons olive oil
- 1 tablespoon lemon juice

TAHINI SAUCE

- 1 cup water
- 1 cup tahini
- 1 garlic clove
- pinch of salt

DIRECTIONS

1. In a blender add garlic, parsley, coriander, lemon juice, onion and blend until smooth
2. Add the remaining ingredients and blend again
3. Form patties and freeze patties for 15-20 minutes
4. In a frying pan place the patties and fry until golden brown
5. When ready transfer patties to a plate and serve with tahini sauce

VEGAN RAMEN

Serves: **6**
Prep Time: **10**   Minutes

Cook Time: **20**   Minutes

Total Time: **30**   Minutes

INGREDIENTS

- 4 cups vegetable broth
- 2 tablespoon soy sauce
- 2 clove garlic
- 1 tsp miso paste
- 1 cup mushrooms
- 1 cup tofu
- 1 cup broccoli florets
- 1 cup ramen noodles
- 1 cup sprouts
- ½ red onion
- ¼ cup cilantro
- 1 tablespoon sesame seeds

DIRECTIONS

1. In a pan sauté garlic, onion and set aside
2. In a pot add broth and sautéed onion, garlic and stir in miso paste

3. Transfer everything to a blender and blend until smooth
4. Add salt soy sauce and blend again
5. In a pan fry mushrooms, noodles, broccoli, sprouts, and tofu
6. Stir in broth and sesame seeds
7. When ready serve fried vegetables with the garlic mixture

Serves: 2
Prep Time: **10**   Minutes

Cook Time: **30**   Minutes

Total Time: **40**   Minutes

INGREDIENTS

- 1 cauliflower head

BBQ SAUCE

- ¼ cup tomato sauce
- 1 tsp garam masala
- 1 tablespoon peanut butter
- 1 tsp olive oil
- 1 tsp Worchester sauce
- 1 tsp soy sauce
- 1 clove garlic
- 1 black pepper

DIRECTIONS

1. In a bowl combine all ingredients for the sauce and whisk well
2. Place the cauliflower in a baking dish and bake for 20-25 minutes at 225 F or until brown
3. When ready remove from the oven and serve with bbq sauce

GARLIC TOFU

Serves: **4**

Prep Time: **10** Minutes

Cook Time: **20** Minutes

Total Time: **30** Minutes

INGREDIENTS

- 1 cup tofu
- 1 cup cooked brown rice
- 1 tablespoon chives
- 1 tablespoon olive oil
- 1 tsp vegan butter
- ¼ cup hoisin sauce
- 1 tablespoon soy sauce
- 2 cloves garlic
- 1 tsp sesame seeds

DIRECTIONS

1. In a bowl combine hoisin sauce, garlic and mix well
2. Add tofu, toss well and refrigerate overnight
3. In a skillet heat olive oil and add tofu and spread on a single layer
4. Add remaining ingredients, sprinkle sesame seeds and cook until browned

5. When ready remove from the pan and serve with brown rice

BUDDHA BOWL

Serves: **4**

Prep Time: **10**   Minutes

Cook Time: **30**   Minutes

Total Time: **40**   Minutes

INGREDIENTS

- 1 cup buckwheat

DRESSING

- 1 tablespoon nutritional yeast
- 1 tsp mustard
- salt
- 1 clove garlic

DIRECTIONS

1. Place the buckwheat into a bowl and add 1-2 cups of water
2. In a blender all the ingredients for the dressing and blend until smooth
3. Divide the buckwheat between 2-3 plates and serve with dressing
4. Add toppings like tomatoes, bell pepper or radish sprouts

VEGAN RICE BACON

Serves: **4**

Prep Time: **10** Minutes

Cook Time: **30** Minutes

Total Time: **40** Minutes

INGREDIENTS

- 2 rice paper sheets
- 1 tablespoon water
- 1 tablespoon olive oil
- 1 tablespoon soy sauce
- ¼ tsp onion powder
- ¼ tsp cumin powder
- 1 tsp tomato sauce
- 1 tsp agave syrup

DIRECTIONS

1. In a bowl combine all ingredients together excepting the rice paper
2. Dip the rice paper into a large plate with water
3. Cut the paper into strips and lay the strips onto a baking tray
4. Brush with sauce from the blender and bake for 10-12 minutes at 300 F
5. When ready remove from the oven and serve

FALAFEL BITES

Serves: **12**
Prep Time: **5**   Minutes

Cook Time: **15**   Minutes

Total Time: **20**   Minutes

INGREDIENTS

-   1 cup chickpeas
-   1 onion
-   ¼ cup parsley
-   2 cloves garlic
-   1 tsp baking soda
-   1 tablespoon flour
-   1 tsp cumin
-   ¼ tsp coriander

DIRECTIONS

1. In a blender add all the ingredients and blend until smooth
2. In a pan heat olive oil and form small patties
3. Cook each falafel until crispy
4. When ready remove and serve

ZUCCHINI FRIES

Serves: **6**

Prep Time: **10**   Minutes

Cook Time: **20**   Minutes

Total Time: **30**   Minutes

INGREDIENTS

- 2 zucchinis
- ¼ cup breadcrumbs
- ¼ cup vegan cheese
- olive oil
- tahini
- pesto
- ketchup

DIRECTIONS

1. Cut zucchinis into thin strips
2. In a bowl add vegan cheese, breadcrumbs, salt and mix well
3. Dip each zucchini strip into the mixture
4. Place the strips onto a parchment paper
5. Bake for 18-20 minutes at 350 F
6. When ready remove from the oven and serve

ZUCCHINI DAL

Serves: 2

Prep Time: 5   Minutes

Cook Time: 20   Minutes

Total Time: 25   Minutes

INGREDIENTS

- 2 cups water
- ½ cup red lentils
- 1 zucchini
- 1 onion
- 2 tablespoons curry powder
- 1 tablespoon olive oil
- salt

DIRECTIONS

1. In a pot add zucchini, onion, pepper and sauté for 5-6 minutes
2. Ad lentils, water and the remaining ingredients
3. Cook on low heat for 15-18 minutes
4. When ready from heat, add scallions and serve

Serves: *12*

Prep Time: 5   Minutes

Cook Time: *15*   Minutes

Total Time: *20*   Minutes

INGREDIENTS

- 2 lb. chickpeas
- ¼ cup parsley
- ½ red onion
- 2 tablespoons yeast flakes
- 2 tablespoons rosemary leaves
- olive oil

DIRECTIONS

1. Place chickpea in a blender and blend until smooth
2. Add remaining ingredients and blend again
3. Remove the mixture from the blender and form small patties
4. Heat olive oil in a pan and fry the patties for 2-3 minutes per side
5. When ready remove from the pan and serve

CRANBERRY SALAD

Serves: **2**
Prep Time: **5**   Minutes

Cook Time: **15**   Minutes

Total Time: **20**   Minutes

INGREDIENTS

- ½ cup celery
- 1 packet Knox Gelatin
- 1 cup cranberry juice
- 1 can berry cranberry sauce
- 1 cup sour cream

DIRECTIONS

1. In a pan add juice, gelatin, cranberry sauce and cook on low heat
2. Add sour cream, celery and continue to cook
3. Pour mixture into a pan
4. Serve when ready

BROCCOLI SALAD

Serves: **2**
Prep Time: **5**   Minutes

Cook Time: **5**   Minutes

Total Time: **10** Minutes

INGREDIENTS

- 1 cup broccoli
- 1 cup quinoa
- 2 radishes
- 2 tablespoons pumpkin seeds
- 1 cup salad dressing

DIRECTIONS

1. **In a bowl combine all ingredients together and mix well**
2. **Serve with dressing**

SUMMER COLESLAW

Serves: **2**

Prep Time: **5** Minutes

Cook Time: **5** Minutes

Total Time: **10** Minutes

INGREDIENTS

- 2 carrots
- 2 purple carrots
- 1 cabbage
- ¼ red onion
- 1 bunch leaves
- 2 kale leaves
- 1 cup salad dressing

DIRECTIONS

1. In a bowl combine all ingredients together and mix well
2. Serve with dressing

MINT SALAD

Serves: **2**

Prep Time: **5**   Minutes

Cook Time: **5**   Minutes

Total Time: **10** Minutes

INGREDIENTS

- 1 lb. broad beans
- ½ lb. peas
- 2 chives
- Mint leaves
- 2 spring onions
- 2 tablespoons olive oil
- 2 tablespoons lemon juice

DIRECTIONS

1. In a bowl combine all ingredients together and mix well
2. Serve with dressing

GRAIN SALAD

Serves: **2**

Prep Time: **5**   Minutes

Cook Time: **5**   Minutes

Total Time: **10** Minutes

INGREDIENTS

- 1 bunch coriander leaves
- 1 bunch mint leaves
- ¼ red onion
- 1 bunch parsley
- 1 cup lentils
- 1 tablespoon pumpkin seeds
- 1 tablespoon pine nuts

DIRECTIONS

1. In a bowl combine all ingredients together and mix well
2. Serve with dressing

CAULIFLOWER SALAD

Serves: **2**

Prep Time: **5**   Minutes

Cook Time: **5**   Minutes

Total Time: **10**   Minutes

INGREDIENTS

- 1 cauliflower
- 4 slices bacon
- ¼ cup sour cream
- ¼ cup mayonnaise
- 1 tablespoon lemon juice
- ¼ tsp garlic powder
- 1 cup cheddar cheese
- ¼ cup chives

DIRECTIONS

1. In a bowl combine all ingredients together and mix well
2. Serve with dressing

CORN SALAD

Serves: **2**

Prep Time: **5**   Minutes

Cook Time: **5**   Minutes

Total Time: **10**   Minutes

INGREDIENTS

- 2 cups corn
- 2 cups tomatoes
- ¼ cup feta
- ¼ red onion
- ¼ cup basil
- 2 tablespoons olive oil
- Juice of ½ lime

DIRECTIONS

1. **In a bowl combine all ingredients together and mix well**
2. **Serve with dressing**

CHICKPEA STEW

Serves: **4**

Prep Time: **15** Minutes

Cook Time: **45** Minutes

Total Time: **60** Minutes

INGREDIENTS

- 2 garlic cloves
- 1 tablespoon olive oil
- 2 scallions
- 1 red bell pepper
- 1 tsp paprika
- 1 tsp cumin
- 3 cups chickpeas
- 3-4 mint leaves
- ½ cup white wine
-

DIRECTIONS

1. Chop all ingredients in big chunks
2. In a large pot heat olive oil and add ingredients one by one
3. Cook for 5-6 or until slightly brown
4. Add remaining ingredients and cook until tender, 35-45 minutes

5. Season while stirring on low heat
6. When ready remove from heat and serve

ONION STEW

Serves: **4**

Prep Time: **15** Minutes

Cook Time: **45** Minutes

Total Time: **60** Minutes

INGREDIENTS

- 2 lb. chicken thighs
- 3-4 tablespoons olive oil
- 2 tablespoons butter
- 3-4 bay leaves
- 5-6 onions
- 3-4 cups chicken broth
- 1 cup cherry tomatoes
- 1 cup spinach

DIRECTIONS

1. Chop all ingredients in big chunks
2. In a large pot heat olive oil and add ingredients one by one
3. Cook for 5-6 or until slightly brown
4. Add remaining ingredients and cook until tender, 35-45 minutes
5. Season while stirring on low heat
6. When ready remove from heat and serve

CASSEROLE RECIPES

CORN CASSEROLE

Serves: **4**

Prep Time: **10**   Minutes

Cook Time: **15**   Minutes

Total Time: **25**   Minutes

INGREDIENTS

- ½ cup cornmeal
- ½ cup butter
- 2 eggs
- 1 cup milk
- ½ cup heavy cream
- 3 cups corn
- ¼ tsp smoked paprika

DIRECTIONS

1. Sauté the veggies and set aside
2. Preheat the oven to 425 F
3. Transfer the sautéed veggies to a baking dish, add remaining ingredients to the baking dish
4. Mix well, add seasoning and place the dish in the oven

5. Bake for 12-15 minutes or until slightly brown
6. When ready remove from the oven and serve

ARTICHOKE CASSEROLE

Serves: *4*

Prep Time: *10*   Minutes

Cook Time: *15*   Minutes

Total Time: *25*   Minutes

INGREDIENTS

- 1 cup cooked rice
- 1 cup milk
- 1 cup parmesan cheese
- 4 oz. cream cheese
- 1 lb. cooked chicken breast
- 1 cup spinach
- 1 can artichoke hearts
- 1 cup mozzarella cheese

DIRECTIONS

1. Sauté the veggies and set aside
2. Preheat the oven to 425 F
3. Transfer the sautéed veggies to a baking dish, add remaining ingredients to the baking dish
4. Mix well, add seasoning and place the dish in the oven
5. Bake for 12-15 minutes or until slightly brown
6. When ready remove from the oven and serve

CASSEROLE PIZZA

Serves: *6-8*

Prep Time: *10*   Minutes

Cook Time: *15*   Minutes

Total Time: *25*   Minutes

INGREDIENTS

- 1 pizza crust
- ½ cup tomato sauce
- ¼ black pepper
- 1 cup zucchini slices
- 1 cup mozzarella cheese
- 1 cup olives

DIRECTIONS

1. Spread tomato sauce on the pizza crust
2. Place all the toppings on the pizza crust
3. Bake the pizza at 425 F for 12-15 minutes
4. When ready remove pizza from the oven and serve

SECOND COOKBOOK

VEGETABLE SOUP

Serves: **8**
Prep Time: **10**   Minutes

Cook Time: **50**   Minutes

Total Time: **60**   Minutes

INGREDIENTS

- 10 cloves garlic
- 2 onion
- ½ lemon
- 2 beets
- 3 carrots
- 1/3 tsp turmeric
- 1/3 tsp oregano
- 1 ½ cup vegetable broth
- 1/3 tsp black pepper
- 2 cups broccoli
- 3 bay leaves
- 1/3 tsp salt

DIRECTIONS

1. **Peel and dice the vegetables**

2. Place in a pot of water and bring to a boil
3. Simmer on low for at least 50 minutes
4. Season and serve hot

PARSNIP SOUP

Serves: *8*

Prep Time: *10*   Minutes

Cook Time: *50*   Minutes

Total Time: *60*   Minutes

INGREDIENTS

- 2 cups vegetable broth
- 2 bay leaves
- 1 tsp salt
- 2 lbs parsnip
- 1/3 cup olive oil
- 1/3 tsp black pepper
- 1 onion
- 1 stalk celery

DIRECTIONS

1. Scrub and cut the parsnip as you desire
2. Place on a baking sheet and toss with oil, salt and pepper
3. Roast until golden
4. Cook the onion and the celery in hot oil for about 5 minutes then season
5. Pour the vegetable broth over, add the bay leaves and the parsnip in and bring to a boil

6. Once boiling, simmer for 15 minutes
7. Remove the bay leaves and puree the soup using a blender
8. Season and serve

ASPARAGUS SOUP

Serves: **6**

Prep Time: **5**   Minutes

Cook Time: **25**   Minutes

Total Time: **30**   Minutes

INGREDIENTS

- 2 leeks
- 1 onion
- 5 tbs flour
- 2 potatoes
- 1/3 tsp nutmeg
- 2 lb asparagus
- 5 cups vegetable stock
- 1 ½ stalk celery
- Salt
- Pepper

DIRECTIONS

1. Cut the asparagus tips off, and set aside, chopped while cutting the asparagus stalks into desired size pieces
2. Simmer the leeks, potatoes, celery, asparagus and onions in vegetable stock for 15 minutes, covered
3. Add the flour and process the soup using a blender

4. Add the remaining vegetable stock, season and simmer covered for 5 minutes

5. Serve immediately

Serves: *4*
Prep Time: *10*   Minutes

Cook Time: *50*   Minutes

Total Time: *60*   Minutes

INGREDIENTS

- 3 cups vegetable stock
- 2 tbs butter
- 4 onions
- 2 cloves garlic
- 4 slices sourdough
- 2 glasses of white wine
- Thyme
- Salt

DIRECTIONS

1. Peel the onions and slice it thinly
2. Cook the onions in melted butter for a few minutes, then add the garlic, thyme, salt and pepper
3. Cook for another 10 minutes
4. Pour the vegetable stock over and allow to simmer covered for at least 40 minutes
5. Add the wine and continue simmering for another 10 minutes

6. Ladle the soup into bowls and cover with the sourdough bread slices

7. Grill for 5 minutes in the preheated grill at 350F

8. Serve immediately

ZUCCHINI SOUP

Serves: **4**

Prep Time: **10**   Minutes

Cook Time: **20**   Minutes

Total Time: **30**   Minutes

INGREDIENTS

- 1 tablespoon olive oil
- 1 lb. zucchini
- ¼ red onion
- ½ cup all-purpose flour
- ¼ tsp salt
- ¼ tsp pepper
- 1 can vegetable broth
- 1 cup heavy cream

DIRECTIONS

1. In a saucepan heat olive oil and sauté zucchini until tender
2. Add remaining ingredients to the saucepan and bring to a boil
3. When all the vegetables are tender transfer to a blender and blend until smooth
4. Pour soup into bowls, garnish with parsley and serve

SIDE DISHES

GARLIC SALMON

Serves: *4*

Prep Time: *10* Minutes

Cook Time: *20* Minutes

Total Time: *30* Minutes

INGREDIENTS

- 2 lb salmon
- 2 tbs water
- Salt
- 2 tbs parsley
- 4 cloves garlic

DIRECTIONS

1. Preheat the oven to 400F.
2. Mix the garlic, parsley, salt and water in a bowl.
3. Brush the mixture over the salmon.
4. Place the fish on a baking tray and cover with aluminum foil.
5. Cook for 20 minutes.
6. Serve with vegetables.

Serves: **4**

Prep Time: **10**   Minutes

Cook Time: **0**   Minutes

Total Time: **10**   Minutes

INGREDIENTS

- **6 ounces tuna**
- **2 tsp yogurt**
- **½ celery stalk**
- **Handful baby spinach**
- **½ onion**
- **2 tsp lemon juice**
- **4 tortillas**

DIRECTIONS

1. **Mix all of the ingredients except for the tortillas in a bowl.**
2. **Spread the mixture over the tortillas, then wrap them up.**
3. **Serve immediately.**

ROASTED CHICKEN WRAP

Serves: **4**

Prep Time: **10** Minutes

Cook Time: **10** Minutes

Total Time: **20** Minutes

INGREDIENTS

- **1 cup chicken breast**
- **2 tsp yogurt**
- **1/3 cup celery**
- **8 tomato slices**
- **½ onion**
- **1 tbs mustard**
- **2 tbs ketchup**
- **4 tortillas**

DIRECTIONS

1. Cut the chicken as you desire and grill until done on each side.
2. Mix all of the ingredients except for the tortillas in a bowl.
3. Spread the mixture over the tortillas and add the chicken.
4. Serve immediately.

Serves: **4**

Prep Time: **10**   Minutes

Cook Time: **0**   Minutes

Total Time: **10**   Minutes

INGREDIENTS

- **1 cup cooked lentils**
- **1 cup baby spinach**
- **1 poached egg**
- **¼ avocado**
- **½ tomato**
- **1-2 slices whole wheat bread**

DIRECTIONS

1. **Mix all of the ingredients together except for the bread.**
2. **Toast the bread.**
3. **Serve immediately together.**

STUFFED EGGPLANT

Serves: **4**

Prep Time: **10** Minutes

Cook Time: **50** Minutes

Total Time: **60** Minutes

INGREDIENTS
- 1 eggplant
- 2 onions
- 1 red pepper
- ½ cup tomato juice
- ¼ cup cheese

DIRECTIONS

1. Preheat the oven to 350F.
2. Cut the eggplant in half and cook for 30 minutes.
3. Cook the diced onion in 2 tbs of water until brown.
4. Add the pepper and add it to the onion, cooking for another 5 minutes.
5. Add the tomato juice and allow to cook for another 5 minutes.
6. Scoop out the eggplant.
7. Mix the eggplant with the onion mixture, then add it back into the eggplant shell.
8. Grate the cheese on top and bake for another 10 minutes.

GARLICKY TOFU

Serves: *4*

Prep Time: *10*   Minutes

Cook Time: *10*   Minutes

Total Time: *20*   Minutes

INGREDIENTS

- 2 tablespoons olive oil
- 2 tablespoons crushed garlic
- salt
- 12-oz. tofu
- black pepper

DIRECTIONS

1. Cut tofu in 1-inch cubes and place in a bowl with olive oil, pepper and garlic
2. In a pan add the tofu mixture and sauté for 5-6 minutes
3. Remove and serve

Serves: *4*
Prep Time: *20* Minutes

Cook Time: *30* Minutes

Total Time: *50* Minutes

INGREDIENTS

- **4 tablespoons olive oil**
- **1 egg**
- **½ tsp cumin**
- **½ tsp turmeric**
- **¼ tsp paprika**
- **1 onion**
- **¼ cup fresh parsley leaves**
- **1 tablespoons Worcestershire sauce**
- **2 lbs. fatty ground beef**
- **¼ lb. duck**
- **¼ cup bread crumbs**

DIRECTIONS

1. **In a skillet heat oil over medium heat, add onions sauté for 2-3 minutes, transfer to a bowl and add parsley and Worcestershire sauce**

2. Add ground beef, livers, eggs, paprika, turmeric, cumin and mix well, add salt and pepper

3. Preheat oven to 400, place the meatballs on a baking sheet

4. Bake for 15-20 minutes, garnish with cheese and serve

ITALIAN PATE WITH FRIED ANCHOVIES

Serves: **10**
Prep Time: **10**   Minutes

Cook Time: **30**   Minutes

Total Time: **40**   Minutes

INGREDIENTS

- 1 ½ lb. chicken liver
- ½ cup avocado oil
- 2 shallots
- 1 garlic clove
- 1 oz. anchovy fillet
- ½ cup capers
- 1 tsp ground sage
- 1 tsp lemon zest
- 1 tablespoon lemon juice

DIRECTIONS

1. Trim your chicken livers and any piece of fat
2. Place the trimmed chicken livers into a bowl, smash cloves
3. Drain the anchovy fillets
4. In a skillet add oil, garlic, shallots, anchovy fillets and capers
5. Cook until golden brown and sprinkle with sage

6. Remove skillet from heat and transfer to a blender, add lemon zest, lemon juice

7. Taste and pour pate into a dish

VEGETABLE FRITTATA

Serves: **4**

Prep Time: **15** Minutes

Cook Time: **20** Minutes

Total Time: **35** Minutes

INGREDIENTS

- 2 egg
- 3 egg whites
- ½ cup parmesan cheese
- 1 tsp turmeric
- ¼ cup orange bell pepper
- ¼ cup red onion
- 1 tsp garlic
- ¼ tsp olive oil
- 1 cup spinach
- salt

DIRECTIONS

1. Whisk the egg whites and eggs in a bowl
2. Add garlic, bell pepper, red onion, parmesan, turmeric and mix well
3. In a pan add egg mixture and spinach leaves
4. Season with salt and pepper and serve

CHICKEN LIVER PATE

Serves: **4**

Prep Time: **10** Minutes

Cook Time: **15** Minutes

Total Time: **25** Minutes

INGREDIENTS

- 1 lb. chicken livers
- ¼ lb. butter
- 1 tablespoons brandy
- 2 tablespoons heavy cream
- 1 orange zest

DIRECTIONS

1. Remove the fat and cut each liver in half
2. In a saucepan melt butter, add chicken livers and cook for 10-12 minutes
3. Remove from heat add brandy, orange zest, orange juice and cream
4. Puree until smooth and season with salt
5. Pour into ramekin dishes and serve

Serves: **4**

Prep Time: **10**   Minutes

Cook Time: **15**   Minutes

Total Time: **25**   Minutes

INGREDIENTS

- **1 lb. chicken livers**
- **1 tsp oil**
- **¼ salt**
- **¼ tsp pepper**
- **4 green onions**
- **1 cup kale pieces**
- **1 cup water**
- **½ cup lemon juice**

DIRECTIONS

1. **In a skillet heat oil over medium heat and add chicken livers and sprinkle with salt**
2. **Cook for 5-10 minutes**
3. **Remove and to a plate**
4. **In the skillet add kale, water and green onions, bring to boil**
5. **Slice the livers, return to the skillet and add lemon juice, serve when ready**

DANISH LIVER PATE

Serves: **4**

Prep Time: **10** Minutes

Cook Time: **50** Minutes

Total Time: **60** Minutes

INGREDIENTS

- 1 lb. liver
- 2/3 lb. bacon bits
- 1 tsp salt
- 1 tsp pepper
- 1 egg
- 1 tablespoon flour
- 4 oz. milk

DIRECTIONS

1. Preheat oven to 200 F
2. In a blender add bacon, onion and liver and blend until smooth
3. Add the rest of the ingredients and mix well
4. Pour mixture into a greased loaf pan
5. Bake for 50-60 minutes
6. Remove and serve

Serves: **4**

Prep Time: **10** Minutes

Cook Time: **20** Minutes

Total Time: **30** Minutes

INGREDIENTS

- 1 lb. chicken breast
- 1 onion
- 1 red pepper
- 1 tomato
- 1 can kidney beans
- 2 cloves garlic
- 1 cup salsa
- 1 bunch broccoli
- cilantro
- olive oil
- salt

DIRECTIONS

1. In a skillet sauté garlic, onion, add pepper and cook for 2-3 minutes
2. Add pepper, bring mixture to boil
3. Reduce the heat and simmer 5-6 minutes

4. Remove and serve with chicken

SPAGHETTI SQUASH HASH BROWNS

Serves: **4**

Prep Time: **10** Minutes

Cook Time: **15** Minutes

Total Time: **25** Minutes

INGREDIENTS

- 2 cups shredded squash
- 1 tablespoon oil

DIRECTIONS

1. In a skillet heat oil over medium heat
2. Remove water out of the squash
3. Place the patties on the skillet and cook for 6-7 minutes
4. Remove and transfer to a paper towel

Serves: **4**

Prep Time: **10** Minutes

Cook Time: **40** Minutes

Total Time: **50** Minutes

INGREDIENTS

- 2 lb. chicken pieces
- 2 lb. pumpkin
- 1 tablespoon paprika powder
- ½ cup pine nuts
- 1 spring rosemary
- 2 tablespoons olive oil
- salt

DIRECTIONS

1. Preheat oven to 375 F and place the chicken into an oven dish
2. Brush with olive oil and add pumpkin
3. Sprinkle salt, paprika, rosemary and bake for 25-30 minutes
4. Remove, add pine nuts and cook for another 5-10 minutes

GREEN PESTO PASTA

Serves: **2**

Prep Time: **5** Minutes

Cook Time: **15** Minutes

Total Time: **20** Minutes

INGREDIENTS

- 4 oz. spaghetti
- 2 cups basil leaves
- 2 garlic cloves
- ¼ cup olive oil
- 2 tablespoons parmesan cheese
- ½ tsp black pepper

DIRECTIONS

1. Bring water to a boil and add pasta
2. In a blend add parmesan cheese, basil leaves, garlic and blend
3. Add olive oil, pepper and blend again
4. Pour pesto onto pasta and serve when ready

CRANBERRY SALAD

Serves: **2**

Prep Time: **5** Minutes

Cook Time: **15** Minutes

Total Time: **20** Minutes

INGREDIENTS

- ½ cup celery
- 1 packet Knox Gelatin
- 1 cup cranberry juice
- 1 can berry cranberry sauce
- 1 cup sour cream

DIRECTIONS

1. In a pan add juice, gelatin, cranberry sauce and cook on low heat
2. Add sour cream, celery and continue to cook
3. Pour mixture into a pan
4. Serve when ready

POTATO SALAD

Serves: 2

Prep Time: 5   Minutes

Cook Time: *10*   Minutes

Total Time: *15*   Minutes

INGREDIENTS

- 5 potatoes
- 1 tsp cumin seeds
- 1/3 cup oil
- 2 tsp mustard
- 1 red onion
- 2 cloves garlic
- 1/3 cup lemon juice
- 1 tsp sea salt

DIRECTIONS

1. Steam the potatoes until tender
2. Mix mustard, turmeric powder, lemon juice, cumin seeds, and salt
3. Place the potatoes in a bowl and pour the lemon mixture over
4. Add the chopped onion and minced garlic over
5. Stir to coat and refrigerate covered
6. Add oil and stir before serving

CARROT SALAD

Serves: **2**

Prep Time: **5**   Minutes

Cook Time: **5**   Minutes

Total Time: **10**   Minutes

INGREDIENTS

- 1 ½ tbs lemon juice
- 1/3 tsp salt
- ¼ tsp black pepper
- 2 tbs olive oil
- 1/3 lb carrots
- 1 tsp mustard

DIRECTIONS

1. Mix mustard, lemon juice and oil together
2. Peel and shred the carrots in a bowl
3. Stir in the dressing and season with salt and pepper
4. Mix well and allow to chill for at least 30 minutes
5. Serve

MOROCCAN SALAD

Serves: *2*

Prep Time: *5*   Minutes

Cook Time: *5*   Minutes

Total Time: *10* Minutes

INGREDIENTS

- 2 tbs lemon juice
- 1 tsp cumin
- 1 tsp paprika
- 3 tbs olive oil
- 2 cloves garlic
- 5 carrots
- Salt
- Pepper

DIRECTIONS

1. Peel and slice the carrots
2. Add the carrots in boiled water and simmer for at least 5 minutes
3. Drain and rinse the carrots under cold water
4. Add in a bowl
5. Mix the lemon juice, garlic, cumin, paprika, and olive oil together

6. Pour the mixture over the carrots and toss then season with salt and pepper
7. Serve immediately

AVOCADO CHICKEN SALAD

Serves: 2

Prep Time: 5   Minutes

Cook Time: 5   Minutes

Total Time: **10**   Minutes

INGREDIENTS

- 3 tsp lime juice
- 3 tbs cilantro
- 1 chicken breast
- 1 avocado
- 1/3 cup onion
- 1 apple
- 1 cup celery
- Salt
- Pepper
- Olive oil

DIRECTIONS

1. Dice the chicken breast
2. Season with salt and pepper and cook into a greased skillet until golden
3. Dice the vegetables and place over the chicken in a bowl
4. Mash the avocado and sprinkle in the cilantro

5. Season with salt and pepper and add lime juice
6. Serve drizzled with olive oil

CUCUMBER SALAD

Serves: *8*

Prep Time: *5*   Minutes

Cook Time: *5*   Minutes

Total Time: *10*   Minutes

INGREDIENTS

- 2 cucumbers
- ½ cup vinegar
- 2 tsp sugar
- 1/3 cup water
- 2 tbs sour cream
- ½ tbs salt
- 1 ½ tsp paprika
- ½ onion

DIRECTIONS

1. Peel and slice the cucumbers
2. Place the cucumbers on a baking sheet and sprinkle with salt
3. Allow to chill for about 30 minutes then squeeze out the excess water
4. Place the onion slices in a bowl and add the drained cucumbers over
5. Add water, sugar, vinegar and paprika

6. Allow to marinate for at least 2 hours

Serves: **2**

Prep Time: **5**   Minutes

Cook Time: **5**   Minutes

Total Time: **10**   Minutes

INGREDIENTS

- 2 red chicory
- 2 fennel bulbs
- ½ cup watercress
- 2 garlic cloves
- 1 tablespoon olive oil

DIRECTIONS

1. **In a bowl combine all ingredients together and mix well**
2. **Serve with dressing**

FENNEL SALAD

Serves: 2

Prep Time: 5   Minutes

Cook Time: 5   Minutes

Total Time: 10   Minutes

INGREDIENTS

- 1 fennel bulb
- 1 tablespoon lemon juice
- ¼ cup olive oil
- 1 tsp mint
- 1 tsp onion

DIRECTIONS

1. In a bowl combine all ingredients together and mix well
2. Serve with dressing

ASPARAGUS FRITATTA

Serves: **2**

Prep Time: **10** Minutes

Cook Time: **20** Minutes

Total Time: **30** Minutes

INGREDIENTS

- ½ lb. asparagus
- 1 tablespoon olive oil
- ½ red onion
- ¼ tsp salt
- 2 oz. cheddar cheese
- 1 garlic clove
- ¼ tsp dill

DIRECTIONS

1. Boil the asparagus until tender and set aside
2. In a bowl whisk eggs with salt and cheese
3. In a frying pan heat olive oil and pour egg mixture
4. Add remaining ingredients and mix well
5. When ready serve with asparagus

SQUASH FRITATTA

Serves:　　　**2**

Prep Time:　**10**　Minutes

Cook Time:　**20**　Minutes

Total Time:　**30**　Minutes

INGREDIENTS

- ½ lb. squash
- 1 tablespoon olive oil
- ½ red onion
- ¼ tsp salt
- 2 oz. cheddar cheese
- 1 garlic clove
- ¼ tsp dill

DIRECTIONS

1. In a bowl whisk eggs with salt and cheese
2. In a frying pan heat olive oil and pour egg mixture
3. Add remaining ingredients and mix well
4. Serve when ready

KALE FRITATTA

Serves: **2**

Prep Time: **10**   Minutes

Cook Time: **20**   Minutes

Total Time: **30**   Minutes

INGREDIENTS

- 1 cup kale
- 1 tablespoon olive oil
- ½ red onion
- ¼ tsp salt
- 2 oz. cheddar cheese
- 1 garlic clove
- ¼ tsp dill

DIRECTIONS

1. In a skillet sauté kale until tender
2. In a bowl whisk eggs with salt and cheese
3. In a frying pan heat olive oil and pour egg mixture
4. Add remaining ingredients and mix well
5. When ready serve with sautéed kale

SPROUTS FRITATTA

Serves: **2**

Prep Time: **10**   Minutes

Cook Time: **20**   Minutes

Total Time: **30**   Minutes

INGREDIENTS

- ½ lb. sprouts
- 1 tablespoon olive oil
- ½ red onion
- ¼ tsp salt
- 2 oz. parmesan cheese
- 1 garlic clove
- ¼ tsp dill

DIRECTIONS

1. In a bowl whisk eggs with salt and parmesan cheese
2. In a frying pan heat olive oil and pour egg mixture
3. Add remaining ingredients and mix well
4. Serve when ready

BROCCOLI FRITATTA

Serves:	**2**
Prep Time:	**10** Minutes
Cook Time:	**20** Minutes
Total Time:	**30** Minutes

INGREDIENTS

- 1 cup broccoli
- 1 tablespoon olive oil
- ½ red onion
- ¼ tsp salt
- 2 oz. cheddar cheese
- 1 garlic clove
- ¼ tsp dill

DIRECTIONS

1. In a skillet sauté broccoli until tender
2. In a bowl whisk eggs with salt and cheese
3. In a frying pan heat olive oil and pour egg mixture
4. Add remaining ingredients and mix well
5. When ready serve with sautéed broccoli

Serves: **3-4**
Prep Time: **10**   Minutes

Cook Time: **20**   Minutes

Total Time: **30**   Minutes

INGREDIENTS

- 2 delicata squashes
- 2 tablespoons olive oil
- 1 tsp curry powder
- 1 tsp salt

DIRECTIONS

1. the oven to 400 F
2. Cut everything in half lengthwise
3. Toss everything with olive oil and place onto a prepared baking sheet
4. Roast for 18-20 minutes at 400 F or until golden brown
5. When ready remove from the oven and serve

PIZZA

ZUCCHINI PIZZA

Serves: **6-8**

Prep Time: **10**   Minutes

Cook Time: **15**   Minutes

Total Time: **25**   Minutes

INGREDIENTS

- 1 pizza crust
- ½ cup tomato sauce
- ¼ black pepper
- 1 cup zucchini slices
- 1 cup mozzarella cheese
- 1 cup olives

DIRECTIONS

1. Spread tomato sauce on the pizza crust
2. Place all the toppings on the pizza crust
3. Bake the pizza at 425 F for 12-15 minutes
4. When ready remove pizza from the oven and serve

ALSATIAN PIZZA

Serves: *6-8*
Prep Time: *10*   Minutes

Cook Time: *15*   Minutes

Total Time: *25*   Minutes

INGREDIENTS

- 1 pizza crust
- 1 cup mozzarella
- ¼ cup sour cream
- ½ red onion
- 4-5 slices bacon
- 1 tsp thyme leaves

DIRECTIONS

1. Spread tomato sauce on the pizza crust
2. Place all the toppings on the pizza crust
3. Bake the pizza at 425 F for 12-15 minutes
4. When ready remove pizza from the oven and serve

VEGAN PIZZA

Serves: **6-8**
Prep Time: **10**   Minutes

Cook Time: **15**   Minutes

Total Time: **25**   Minutes

INGREDIENTS

- 1 pizza crust
- 2 cloves garlic
- 1 cup sweetcorn
- 1 tsp smoked paprika
- 1 cup mushrooms
- 1 cup onion

DIRECTIONS

1. Spread tomato sauce on the pizza crust
2. Place all the toppings on the pizza crust
3. Bake the pizza at 425 F for 12-15 minutes
4. When ready remove pizza from the oven and serve

Serves: *6-8*
Prep Time: *10* Minutes

Cook Time: *15* Minutes

Total Time: *25* Minutes

INGREDIENTS

- 1 pizza crust
- 1 pack salami
- 4 oz. taleggio
- 2 tablespoons mascarpone
- 3 oz. kale
- 2 cloves garlic
- 1 red onion

DIRECTIONS

1. Spread tomato sauce on the pizza crust
2. Place all the toppings on the pizza crust
3. Bake the pizza at 425 F for 12-15 minutes
4. When ready remove pizza from the oven and serve

HALLOUMI PIZZA

Serves: *6-8*

Prep Time: *10*   Minutes

Cook Time: *15*   Minutes

Total Time: *25*   Minutes

INGREDIENTS

- 4 roasted red pepper
- 2 sundried tomatoes
- 1 pizza crust
- 1 tsp cumin
- 1 tsp paprika
- 1 cup tomato sauce
- ½ lb. halloumi
- 1 tablespoon olive oil
- ¼ lb. walnuts

DIRECTIONS

1. Spread tomato sauce on the pizza crust
2. Place all the toppings on the pizza crust
3. Bake the pizza at 425 F for 12-15 minutes
4. When ready remove pizza from the oven and serve

BROCCOLI PIZZA

Serves: *6-8*
Prep Time: *10*   Minutes

Cook Time: *15*   Minutes

Total Time: *25*   Minutes

INGREDIENTS

- 1 pizza crust
- ½ lb. broccoli
- 2 pork saausages
- 1 clove garlic
- 1 tablespoon olive oil
- ½ lb. taleggio

DIRECTIONS

1. Spread tomato sauce on the pizza crust
2. Place all the toppings on the pizza crust
3. Bake the pizza at 425 F for 12-15 minutes
4. When ready remove pizza from the oven and serve

KALE PIZZA

Serves: **6-8**

Prep Time: **10**   Minutes

Cook Time: **15**   Minutes

Total Time: **25**   Minutes

INGREDIENTS

- 1 pizza crust
- 2 pork sausages
- 2 tsp fennel seeds
- 1 tsp smoked paprika
- 2 cloves garlic
- ½ lb taleggio
- 1 cup mozzarella

DIRECTIONS

1. Spread tomato sauce on the pizza crust
2. Place all the toppings on the pizza crust
3. Bake the pizza at 425 F for 12-15 minutes
4. When ready remove pizza from the oven and serve

THIRD COOKBOOK

BREAKFAST RECIPES

EGG MUFFINS WITH CHEESE

Serves: *4*

Prep Time: *10* Minutes

Cook Time: *20* Minutes

Total Time: *30* Minutes

INGREDIENTS

- ¼ cup red pepper
- ¼ zucchini
- 1 tablespoon jalapeno
- 6 eggs
- 1 cup cheddar cheese
- ¼ tsp salt
- ¼ cup red onions

DIRECTIONS

1. Preheat oven to 375 F and place 6 baking cups inside muffin tin
2. In a bowl mix zucchini, cheese, eggs, salt, pepper ad jalapeno
3. Divide the mixture between you baking cups and bake for 15-20 minutes

BLUEBERRY MUFFINS

Serves: *8*

Prep Time: *10* Minutes

Cook Time: *30* Minutes

Total Time: *40* Minutes

INGREDIENTS

- 2 cups almond flour
- 2 eggs
- ½ tsp cream tartar
- ¼ tsp baking soda
- ¼ tsp salt
- 1 cup blueberries
- ¼ tsp vanilla extract
- ½ cup arrowroot flour
- ½ cup maple syrup

DIRECTIONS

1. Preheat oven to 325 F
2. In a bowl mix all the flour ingredients, salt and baking soda
3. Add maple syrup, vanilla extract, eggs and stir
4. Add blueberries and pour over parchment paper and bake for 20 minutes

LEMON MUFFINS

Serves: *8*

Prep Time: *15* Minutes

Cook Time: *30* Minutes

Total Time: *45* Minutes

INGREDIENTS

- 2 cups almond flour
- ¼ tsp salt
- zest of one lemon
- 1 tablespoon poppy seeds
- ¼ baking soda
- 1 tablespoon coconut flour
- 4 eggs
- ¼ cup honey
- 1 tsp sucanat
- ¾ tsp vanilla extract
- 1 tsp lemon extract

DIRECTIONS

1. Preheat oven to 325 F and grease muffin cups with coconut oil
2. In a bowl mix almond and coconut flour, salt, baking soda and poppy seeds
3. In another bowl whisk together lemon extract, zest, eggs, vanilla, honey and pour the mixture into muffin cups
4. Mix almond flour with sucanat and sprinkle over the muffins

5. Bake for 20-25 minutes, remove when ready and serve

FRENCH TOAST

Serves: **2**

Prep Time: **10** Minutes

Cook Time: **40** Minutes

Total Time: **50** Minutes

INGREDIENTS

- ½ cup butter
- ½ cup applesauce
- 1 tablespoon honey
- ¼ tsp salt
- 5 eggs
- ¼ cup coconut flour

DIRECTIONS

1. Preheat oven to 325 F and grease one pan with butter
2. In a bowl mix eggs, salt, honey, apple sauce, coconut flour, salt and pour the batter into the pan
3. Bake for 35-40 minutes until bread is brown
4. Remove the pan and let it cool before serving

QUICHE WITH BACON AND TOMATO

Serves: *4*

Prep Time: *15* Minutes

Cook Time: *30* Minutes

Total Time: *45* Minutes

INGREDIENTS

- 10 eggs
- 6 oz. cheese
- ¼ tsp salt
- ¼ tsp pepper
- 1 potato
- 5 strips of bacon
- ¼ cup green onion
- ¼ cup tomato

DIRECTIONS

1. Preheat oven to 3250 F
2. In a skillet fry bacon for 5-10 minutes and remove when ready
3. In a skillet place potato slices
4. In a bowl whisk eggs, grate cheese and mix with pepper, tomato, onion and salt
5. Pour the mixture into skillet
6. Place the skillet in the oven and bake for 20 minutes

APPLE FRITTER

Serves: *4*

Prep Time: *10* Minutes

Cook Time: *30* Minutes

Total Time: *40* Minutes

INGREDIENTS

- 2 apples
- ¼ tsp lemon juice
- 1 tsp cinnamon
- 1 tablespoon maple sugar

Dough

- 1 egg
- ¼ tsp cinnamon
- ¼ tsp nutmeg
- sal
- ¼ cup arrowroot flour
- ¼ tsp maple sugar
- 1 tsp maple syrup

DIRECTIONS

1. In a bowl place the apples with cinnamon, maple syrup, lemon juice and coconut sugar

2. In another bowl mix, nutmeg, cinnamon, salt, maple sugar, arrowroot flour

3. In a skillet heat oil and add the apples to the dough mixture and then place into skillet

4. Cook 2-3 minutes each side each apple slice

5. Remove and serve

BREAKFAST SAUSAGE

Serves: **4**

Prep Time: **10** Minutes

Cook Time: **10** Minutes

Total Time: **20** Minutes

INGREDIENTS

- 1-pound lean pork
- 1 tablespoon maple syrup
- 1 tsp Italian seasoning
- 1 tsp salt
- ¼ tsp thyme

DIRECTIONS

1. In a bowl mix all the ingredients
2. Form into patties and fry in a skillet
3. Remove when golden brown and serve

ALMOND FLOUR PANCAKES

Serves: *4*

Prep Time: *10* Minutes

Cook Time: *20* Minutes

Total Time: *30* Minutes

INGREDIENTS

- 1 cup almond flour
- 1 egg
- 1tsp vanilla extract
- ¼ tsp baking soda
- salt
- ¾ cup milk
- sliced fruits (strawberries, bananas, blueberries)

DIRECTIONS

1. Preheat griddle to 300 F
2. In a bowl whisk together baking soda, salt, almond flour, eggs, milk and vanilla extract
3. Pour the mixture on the griddle and cook each pancake for2-3 minutes per side
4. Remove and serve with fruit and maple syrup on top

BLUEBERRY PANCAKES

Serves: *8*

Prep Time: *10* Minutes

Cook Time: *10* Minutes

Total Time: *20* Minutes

INGREDIENTS

- 1 cups buckwheat flour
- 1 cups water
- ¼ tsp baking soda
- ¼ tsp salt
- 1 cups blueberry
- juice from 2 lemons
- ½ cup tapioca flour
- 1 egg
- ¼ cup avocado oil
- 2 tablespoons cane sugar
- 2 tsp almond extract
- 1 tsp baking powder

DIRECTIONS

1. Make the pancakes mixture the night before cooking
2. In a bowl mix buckwheat flour, lemon juice, water and stir
3. In the morning add the rest of the ingredients in the mixture

4. In a skillet pour the pancakes mixture and cook 2-3 minutes per side

BACON AND EGG BREAKFAST

Serves: **4**

Prep Time: **10** Minutes

Cook Time: **40** Minutes

Total Time: **50** Minutes

INGREDIENTS

- 1 8-ounce bacon package
- 2 eggs
- coconut oil
- mushrooms

DIRECTIONS

1. **Preheat oven to 350 F**
2. **Grease 4 muffin thin and then line the walls of the muffin cup with with a bacon strip, bake for 10-12 minutes**
3. **In a bowl whisk together the eggs with garlic, tomatoes, cheese, spinach and mushrooms**
4. **Pour the mixture in the muffin cup and bake for 25-30 minutes**
5. **When ready remove from the oven and serve**

MAPLE GRANOLA

Serves: **4**

Prep Time: **10** Minutes

Cook Time: **30** Minutes

Total Time: **40** Minutes

INGREDIENTS

- 1 cup almond slivers
- ½ tsp salt
- 1 cup coconut flakes
- 5 tablespoons male syrup
- 1 cup sunflower seeds
- 1 cup pecans
- 1 tablespoon vanilla extract
- 1 tsp cinnamon

DIRECTIONS

1. Preheat oven to 300 F and line a baking sheet with parchment paper
2. In a bowl place coconut flakes, pecans, sunflower seeds, almond sliver and mix
3. In another bowl mix vanilla extract, maple syrup, salt and cinnamon
4. Pour the mixture into the pan and bake for 35-40 minutes
5. When ready remove and cut into smaller pieces and serve

GRAIN PORRIDGE

Serves: *4*

Prep Time: *10*   Minutes

Cook Time: *50*   Minutes

Total Time: *60*   Minutes

INGREDIENTS

- 1 cup oats
- ½ cup maple syrup
- 1 tablespoon coconut oil
- ¼ cup currants
- 1 tablespoon fenugreek seeds
- 1 tablespoon fennel seeds
- 1 cup barley
- 1 tsp salt
- 1 cup quinoa
- ½ cup pumpkin seeds
- 1 tablespoon apple cider vinegar
- 3 eggs
- 1 cup coconut milk

DIRECTIONS

1. In a bowl mix the quinoa, pumpkin seeds, oats and barley
2. Add vinegar and water and stir and allow to soak for 12 hours

3. Heat the oven to 325

4. In a bowl mix coconut oil, maple syrup, eggs and coconut milk

5. Pour the mixture over the soaked grains and stir

6. In a skillet toss the fenugreek and fennel for 2-3 minutes

7. Transfer to the mixing bowl and pour the mixture into a baking dish

8. Bake for 45-50 minutes and remove when golden brown

9. Serve with yogurt or maple syrup

PUMPKIN SPICE GRANOLA

Serves: *4*

Prep Time: *10* Minutes

Cook Time: *30* Minutes

Total Time: *40* Minutes

INGREDIENTS

- 3 cups oats
- 1 cup water
- ¼ cup ghee
- ¼ cup butter
- ¼ cup raisins
- ½ shredded coconut
- ¼ cup yogurt
- ¼ cup pumpkin seeds
- 1 cup nuts
- 1 cup pumpkin puree
- 1 tsp cinnamon powder
- ¼ tsp ginger powder
- ¼ tsp clove powder
- ¼ tsp salt

DIRECTIONS

1. Pour the water over the oats and mix, add yogurt and mix, cover and allow to soak overnight (12 h)
2. In a food processor place the seeds, nuts and blend
3. Add the mixture to the soaked oats
4. In another bowl mix all the ingredients with the pumpkin puree
5. Spread the mixture onto parchment paper lined baking sheets until dry and crispy
6. Remove and serve

PUMPKIN PIE PORRIDGE

Serves: *2*

Prep Time: *10*   Minutes

Cook Time: *50*   Minutes

Total Time: *60*   Minutes

INGREDIENTS

- 1 pie pumpkin
- ½ tsp cloves
- 1 tsp salt
- ¼ cup honey
- 1 cup coconut milk
- 1 tsp cinnamon
- 2 tsp ginger

DIRECTIONS

1. Preheat oven to 325 F
2. Cut pumpkin in half and place the halves in a baking dish
3. Place in the oven and bake for 45 minutes
4. The flesh of the pumpkin blend until smooth and add coconut milk and honey
5. Pour the mixture over the pumpkin and serve

EGGS AND SPINACH

Serves: *4*

Prep Time: *5*   Minutes

Cook Time: *10*   Minutes

Total Time: *15*   Minutes

INGREDIENTS

- 1 ½ tsp chilli flakes
- 4 eggs
- 3 ½ oz spinach
- 1 lb tomatoes

DIRECTIONS

1. Wilt the spinach
2. Squeeze the excess water out
3. Divide among 4 bowls
4. Mix the tomatoes with the seasoning and chilli flakes
5. Add to the spinach bowls
6. Crack an egg into each bowl and bake for about 15 minutes in the preheated oven at 365F

MORNING SAUSAGE

Serves: *4*

Prep Time: *15* Minutes

Cook Time: *35* Minutes

Total Time: *50* Minutes

INGREDIENTS

- 1 lb ground chicken
- 1 ½ tsp smoked paprika
- ½ tsp salt
- 1 ½ tsp rubbed sage
- 1/3 tsp white pepper
- 1/3 tsp thyme
- 1/5 tsp nutmeg
- 1 ½ tbs olive oil

DIRECTIONS

1. Mix the sage, ground meet, paprika, white pepper, nutmeg, thyme and salt
2. Form patties and place them on a baking sheet
3. Fry the patties in hot oil until brown on both sides
4. Serve immediately

BREAKFAST TACO

Serves: *2*

Prep Time: *10*   Minutes

Cook Time: *20*   Minutes

Total Time: *30*   Minutes

INGREDIENTS

- ¼ cup onion
- 1/3 cup green pepper
- 2 tsp sage
- Corn tortillas
- 1 lb turkey
- 1 tsp thyme
- 4 cups eggs
- 2 lb hash browns

DIRECTIONS

1. Mix hash browns and oil, then spread on a baking pan
2. Bake for about 20 minutes until browned
3. Scramble the eggs with onions and peppers
4. Combine the sage and thyme together
5. Fill a tortilla with ½ cup mixture, then microwave for about 15 seconds
6. Serve immediately

STUFFED POTATOES

Serves: **6**

Prep Time: **10**   Minutes

Cook Time: **20**   Minutes

Total Time: **30**   Minutes

INGREDIENTS

- 3 potatoes
- 1/3 cup scallions
- 3 eggs
- 1/3 tsp salt
- 3 tbs butter
- 1/3 tsp pepper
- ½ cup cheese
- ½ cup red pepper

DIRECTIONS

1. Prick potatoes with a fork and microwave for a few minutes until tender
2. Cut the potatoes lengthwise and scoop out the flesh
3. Cook the bell pepper, scallions and chopped potato flesh in melted butter for about 3 minutes
4. Add eggs, salt and pepper and cook 2 more minutes
5. Remove from heat and fold in the cheese

6. Stuff each potato half with the mixture, allow to cool and wrap with foil

7. Refrigerate overnight

8. Cook for about 10 minutes turning once

9. Serve immediately

AVOCADO TOAST

Serves:	*2*	
Prep Time:	*5*	Minutes
Cook Time:	*5*	Minutes
Total Time:	*10*	Minutes

INGREDIENTS

Pesto:

- 1 ½ tbs olive oil
- 1 tbs hot water
- 1/8 tsp black pepper
- ¼ tsp garlic powder
- 1/3 cup basil leaves
- ¼ cup walnuts
- 1 lemon

Toast:

- 1/3 tsp black pepper
- 2 tsp olive oil
- 4 slices bread
- 1 avocado

DIRECTIONS

1. **Place the pesto ingredients into a food processor and pulse until smooth**
2. **Toast the bread**

3. Divide the avocado slices

4. Spread pesto over avocado, then drizzle with lemon juice and olive oil

5. Serve immediately

MORNING BAKE

Serves: **12**

Prep Time: **10** Minutes

Cook Time: **30** Minutes

Total Time: **40** Minutes

INGREDIENTS

- 4 eggs
- 3 cups hash brown
- 12 oz turkey sausage
- 1 bell pepper
- 1 cup cheese
- 2 cups milk
- 1 onion
- ½ tsp salt
- ¼ tsp black pepper

DIRECTIONS

1. Cook the onion, pepper and sausage until done
2. Stir together with frozen potatoes and ½ cup cheese, then place into a baking dish
3. Mix together milk, pepper, salt and eggs and pour over
4. Bake uncovered for about 30 minutes
5. Sprinkle with cheese and bake 2 more minutes

HAM OMELETTE

Serves: **2**

Prep Time: **10**   Minutes

Cook Time: **20**   Minutes

Total Time: **30**   Minutes

INGREDIENTS

- 4 eggs
- 1 tbs paprika
- 2 tbs olive oil
- ½ tbs onion powder
- ½ cup onion
- 1/3 cup ham
- ½ cup red pepper
- ½ tbs garlic powder

DIRECTIONS

1. Sauté the onion in hot oil
2. Add in the red pepper and sauté until roasted on edges
3. Add ham and paprika and cook 2 more minutes
4. Whisk together the eggs in a bowl
5. Scramble the eggs in hot oil in another skillet
6. Sprinkle with onion and garlic powder
7. Place the ham mixture on one half of the omelette and fold it

QUICHE CUPS

Serves: *8*
Prep Time: *10*   Minutes

Cook Time: *30*   Minutes

Total Time: *40*   Minutes

INGREDIENTS

- 10 oz broccoli
- 2 drops hot sauce
- 1/3 tsp black pepper
- 4 eggs
- 1 cup cheese
- ½ cup bell peppers
- 1 green onion

DIRECTIONS

1. Squeeze the vegetables dry
2. Blend the ingredients together using a food processor
3. Divide among a lined muffin pan
4. Bake for about 30 minutes
5. Allow to cool, then serve

CHICKEN SAUSAGE

Serves: **4**

Prep Time: **5** Minutes

Cook Time: **10** Minutes

Total Time: **15** Minutes

INGREDIENTS

- ½ tsp red pepper flakes
- 1 ½ tsp maple syrup
- 3 tsp olive oil
- 1 ½ tsp sage
- 1 ½ tsp garlic powder
- 1 ½ tsp black pepper
- 1 lb. ground chicken

DIRECTIONS

1. Mix everything together except for the oil
2. Form patties from the mixture
3. Cook the patties in hot oil until cooked through
4. Serve immediately

BURRITO BOWL

Serves: **4**

Prep Time: **10** Minutes

Cook Time: **15** Minutes

Total Time: **25** Minutes

INGREDIENTS

- 2 tbs olive oil
- ½ cup almond milk
- 2 tbs shallot
- 1 cup red pepper
- 1/3 cup salsa
- 2 eggs
- 2 egg whites
- ½ cup onion
- 2 avocados
- 15 oz pinto beans
- 2 tsp cumin
- 1 cup cherry tomatoes

DIRECTIONS

1. Sauté the onion until soft
2. Add the red peppers and cook until they are also soft

3. Add chili powder, pinto beans and cumin, cook a little more, then cover and turn the heat off

4. Chop the tomatoes and avocados

5. Combine ½ chopped avocado, shallot, salsa and almond milk in a food processor

6. Pulse until combined

7. Scramble the eggs and egg whites

8. Divide the bean mixture into bowls, top with avocado, tomatoes, eggs and drizzle with avocado sauce

9. Serve immediately

TART RECIPES

HAZELNUT TART

Serves: *6-8*

Prep Time: *25*   Minutes

Cook Time: *25*   Minutes

Total Time: *50*   Minutes

INGREDIENTS

- pastry sheets
- 3 oz. brown sugar
- ¼ lb. hazelnuts
- 100 ml double cream
- 2 tablespoons syrup
- ¼ lb. dark chocolate
- 2 oz. butter

DIRECTIONS

1. Preheat oven to 400 F, unfold pastry sheets and place them on a baking sheet
2. Toss together all ingredients together and mix well
3. Spread mixture in a single layer on the pastry sheets
4. Before baking decorate with your desired fruits
5. Bake at 400 F for 22-25 minutes or until golden brown
6. When ready remove from the oven and serve

PEAR TART

Serves: *6-8*

Prep Time: *25*   Minutes

Cook Time: *25*   Minutes

Total Time: *50*   Minutes

INGREDIENTS

- 1 lb. pears
- 2 oz. brown sugar
- ½ lb. flaked almonds
- ¼ lb. porridge oat
- 2 oz. flour
- ¼ lb. almonds
- pastry sheets
- 2 tablespoons syrup

DIRECTIONS

1. Preheat oven to 400 F, unfold pastry sheets and place them on a baking sheet
2. Toss together all ingredients together and mix well
3. Spread mixture in a single layer on the pastry sheets
4. Before baking decorate with your desired fruits
5. Bake at 400 F for 22-25 minutes or until golden brown
6. When ready remove from the oven and serve

PIE RECIPES

PEACH PECAN PIE

Serves: **8-12**

Prep Time: **15**   Minutes
Cook Time: **35**   Minutes
Total Time: **50**   Minutes

INGREDIENTS

- **4-5 cups peaches**
- **1 tablespoon preserves**
- **1 cup sugar**
- **4 small egg yolks**
- **¼ cup flour**
- **1 tsp vanilla extract**

DIRECTIONS

1. **Line a pie plate or pie form with pastry and cover the edges of the plate depending on your preference**
2. **In a bowl combine all pie ingredients together and mix well**
3. **Pour the mixture over the pastry**
4. **Bake at 400-425 F for 25-30 minutes or until golden brown**
5. **When ready remove from the oven and let it rest for 15 minutes**

GRAPEFRUIT PIE

Serves: **8-12**
Prep Time: **15**   Minutes

Cook Time: **35**   Minutes

Total Time: **50**   Minutes

INGREDIENTS

- pastry sheets
- 2 cups grapefruit
- 1 cup brown sugar
- ¼ cup flour
- 5-6 egg yolks
- 5 oz. butter

DIRECTIONS

1. Line a pie plate or pie form with pastry and cover the edges of the plate depending on your preference
2. In a bowl combine all pie ingredients together and mix well
3. Pour the mixture over the pastry
4. Bake at 400-425 F for 25-30 minutes or until golden brown
5. When ready remove from the oven and let it rest for 15 minutes

BUTTERFINGER PIE

Serves: *8-12*

Prep Time: *15*   Minutes

Cook Time: *35*   Minutes

Total Time: *50*   Minutes

INGREDIENTS

- pastry sheets
- 1 package cream cheese
- 1 tsp vanilla extract
- ¼ cup peanut butter
- 1 cup powdered sugar (to decorate)
- 2 cups Butterfinger candy bars
- 8 oz whipped topping

DIRECTIONS

1. Line a pie plate or pie form with pastry and cover the edges of the plate depending on your preference
2. In a bowl combine all pie ingredients together and mix well
3. Pour the mixture over the pastry
4. Bake at 400-425 F for 25-30 minutes or until golden brown
5. When ready remove from the oven and let it rest for 15 minutes

SMOOTHIE RECIPES

MACA SMOOTHIE

Serves: *1*

Prep Time: *5*   Minutes

Cook Time: *5*   Minutes

Total Time: *10* Minutes

INGREDIENTS

- 2 cups hemp milk
- 1 cup ice
- ¼ cup lemon juice
- 2 mangoes
- 1 tablespoon flaxseeds
- 1 tsp maca power
- 1 tsp vanilla extract

DIRECTIONS

1. In a blender place all ingredients and blend until smooth
2. Pour smoothie in a glass and serve

BABY SPINACH SMOOTHIE

Serves: *1*

Prep Time: *5*   Minutes

Cook Time: *5*   Minutes

Total Time: *10*   Minutes

INGREDIENTS

- 1 cup cherry juice
- 1 cup spinach
- 1 cup vanilla yoghurt
- 1 avocado
- 1 cup berries
- 1 tablespoon chia seeds

DIRECTIONS

1. In a blender place all ingredients and blend until smooth
2. Pour smoothie in a glass and serve

SUNRISE SMOOTHIE

Serves: *1*
Prep Time: *5*   Minutes

Cook Time: *5*   Minutes

Total Time: *10* Minutes

INGREDIENTS

- 1 cup coconut milk
- 1 banana
- ¼ cup lemon juice
- ¼ mango
- 1 tsp almonds
- 1 cup ice

DIRECTIONS

1. **In a blender place all ingredients and blend until smooth**
2. **Pour smoothie in a glass and serve**

CUCUMBER SMOOTHIE

Serves: *1*

Prep Time: *5* Minutes

Cook Time: *5* Minutes

Total Time: *10* Minutes

INGREDIENTS

- 1 cup vanilla yoghurt
- 1 cup cucumber
- 2 tablespoons dill
- 1 tablespoon basil
- 2 tablespoons mint
- 1 cup ice

DIRECTIONS

1. In a blender place all ingredients and blend until smooth
2. Pour smoothie in a glass and serve

CHERRY SMOOTHIE

Serves: *1*

Prep Time: *5*   Minutes

Cook Time: *5*   Minutes

Total Time: *10* Minutes

INGREDIENTS

- 1 can cherries
- 2 tablespoons peanut butter
- 1 tablespoon honey
- 1 cup Greek Yoghurt
- 1 cup coconut milk

DIRECTIONS

1. In a blender place all ingredients and blend until smooth
2. Pour smoothie in a glass and serve

CHOCOLATE SMOOTHIE

Serves: *1*

Prep Time: *5*   Minutes

Cook Time: *5*   Minutes

Total Time: *10* Minutes

INGREDIENTS

- 2 bananas
- 1 cup Greek Yoghurt
- 1 tablespoon honey
- 1 tablespoon cocoa powder
- ½ cup chocolate chips
- ¼ cup almond milk

DIRECTIONS

1. In a blender place all ingredients and blend until smooth
2. Pour smoothie in a glass and serve

TOFU SMOOTHIE

Serves: *1*

Prep Time: *5*   Minutes

Cook Time: *5*   Minutes

Total Time: *10*   Minutes

INGREDIENTS

- 1 cup blueberries
- ¼ cup tofu
- ¼ cup pomegranate juice
- 1 cup ice
- ½ cup agave nectar

DIRECTIONS

1. **In a blender place all ingredients and blend until smooth**
2. **Pour smoothie in a glass and serve**

COCONUT SMOOTHIE

Serves: *1*

Prep Time: *5* Minutes

Cook Time: *5* Minutes

Total Time: *10* Minutes

INGREDIENTS

- 1 cup blueberries
- 2 bananas
- 1 cup coconut flakes
- 1 cup coconut milk
- ¼ tsp vanilla essence

DIRECTIONS

1. In a blender place all ingredients and blend until smooth
2. Pour smoothie in a glass and serve

ICE-CREAM RECIPES

SAFFRON ICE-CREAM

Serves: **6-8**

Prep Time: **15**   Minutes

Cook Time: **15**   Minutes

Total Time: **30**   Minutes

INGREDIENTS

- **4 egg yolks**
- **1 cup heavy cream**
- **1 cup milk**
- **½ cup brown sugar**
- **1 tsp saffron**
- **1 tsp vanilla extract**

DIRECTIONS

1. **In a saucepan whisk together all ingredients**
2. **Mix until bubbly**
3. **Strain into a bowl and cool**
4. **Whisk in favorite fruits and mix well**
5. **Cover and refrigerate for 2-3 hours**
6. **Pour mixture in the ice-cream maker and follow manufacturer instructions**
7. **Serve when ready**

PISTACHIOS ICE-CREAM

Serves: **6-8**

Prep Time: **15**   Minutes

Cook Time: **15**   Minutes

Total Time: **30**   Minutes

INGREDIENTS

- 4 egg yolks
- 1 cup heavy cream
- 1 cup milk
- 1 cup sugar
- 1 vanilla bean
- 1 tsp almond extract
- 1 cup cherries
- ½ cup pistachios

DIRECTIONS

1. In a saucepan whisk together all ingredients
2. Mix until bubbly
3. Strain into a bowl and cool
4. Whisk in favorite fruits and mix well
5. Cover and refrigerate for 2-3 hours
6. Pour mixture in the ice-cream maker and follow manufacturer instructions

FOURTH COOKBOOK

SIDE DISHES

POTATO LATKES RECIPE

Serves: **4**

Prep Time: **10** Minutes

Cook Time: **30** Minutes

Total Time: **40** Minutes

INGREDIENTS

- ½ cup vegetable oil
- 3 baking potatoes
- 1 egg
- ½ cup flour
- ½ cup onion
- ¼ tsp salt
- ¼ tsp black pepper
- 1 tablespoon parsley

DIRECTIONS

1. In a bowl grate the potatoes and add egg, onion, flour, egg, pepper, salt and mix well
2. In a skillet add 1-2 tablespoons of mixture and cook for 2-3 minutes per side or until golden
3. When ready, remove and garnish with parsley

SHEPERD'S PIE RECIPE

Serves: **4**
Prep Time: **10** Minutes

Cook Time: **30** Minutes

Total Time: **40** Minutes

INGREDIENTS

- 2 tablespoons olive oil
- 1 ground turkey
- ¾ cup diced onion
- 2 tsp garlic
- 2 tablespoon flour
- ¼ cup chicken stock
- ¼ cup rice milk
- 1 tablespoon parsley
- 1 cup mashed potatoes
- ½ tsp paprika

DIRECTIONS

1. Preheat the oven to 375 F
2. In a skillet add olive oil, turkey, garlic and olive oil and sauté for 3-4 minutes
3. Add flour, rice milk, chicken stock and mix well
4. Bring to a boil and simmer for 3-4 minutes

5. Add parsley and place mixture into a casserole dish
6. Bake for 30-35 minutes, sprinkle with paprika and serve

HERBED STUFFING

Serves: **4**

Prep Time: **10** Minutes

Cook Time: **30** Minutes

Total Time: **40** Minutes

INGREDIENTS

- 3 tablespoons olive oil
- 1 cup onions
- 1 clove garlic
- ½ tsp sage
- ½ tsp thyme
- ¾ cup cranberry juice
- ¼ cup chicken stock
- 3 cups stuffing croutons

DIRECTIONS

1. Preheat the oven to 325 F
2. In a skillet add garlic, onions, sage and sauté until soft
3. Add chicken stock, cranberry, croutons and bring to a simmer
4. Transfer to a casserole dish and bake for 18-20 minutes
5. When ready, remove and serve

PRETZELS

Serves: **10**

Prep Time: **10** Minutes

Cook Time: **20** Minutes

Total Time: **30** Minutes

INGREDIENTS

- 1 cup water
- 1 package dry active yeast
- 1 cup flour
- 2 tablespoons vegetable oil
- ¼ tsp salt
- 1 cup flour
- 3 cups water
- 2 tablespoons baking soda
- 2 tablespoons salt

DIRECTIONS

1. Preheat the oven to 450 F
2. Dissolve the yeast in a bowl
3. Add flour, salt, vegetable oil and mix well, let the dough rest for 50-60 minutes
4. Divide into 8-10 balls and roll into pretzel shapes

5. Sprinkle with sesame seeds or salt and bake the pretzels for 12-15 minutes

6. When ready remove and serve

TANGY PORK

Serves: **4**

Prep Time: **10** Minutes

Cook Time: **15** Minutes

Total Time: **25** Minutes

INGREDIENTS

- 1 tablespoon water
- 1 tablespoon Worcestershire sauce
- 1 tsp lemon juice
- 1 tsp mustard
- 3 pork top loin chops
- ¼ tsp lemon seasoning
- 1 tablespoon butter
- 1 tablespoon chives

DIRECTIONS

1. In a bowl add lemon juice, Worcestershire sauce, mustard, mix well and set aside
2. Sprinkle chops with lemon seasoning and place chops in a skillet
3. Cook for 10-12 minutes, transfer to a plate and set aside
4. Pour sauce into skillet and chops over sauce
5. Sprinkle with chives
6. When ready, remove and serve

Serves: *4*

Prep Time: *10*   Minutes

Cook Time: *20*   Minutes

Total Time: *30*   Minutes

INGREDIENTS

- ½ lb. beef
- ½ cup oats
- 2 tablespoons milk
- 1 tsp onion flakes
- ¼ tsp canola oil
- 1 dash pepper

DIRECTIONS

1. In a bowl mix all ingredients and form into patties
2. Heat oil in a skillet and cook each burger for 3-4 minutes per side
3. Remove and serve with potato fries

Serves: *4*

Prep Time: *10* Minutes

Cook Time: *20* Minutes

Total Time: *30* Minutes

INGREDIENTS

- ¾ cup marinade
- 12 oz. chicken breast
- 1 lemon
- 3 wedges

DIRECTIONS

1. In a plastic bag marinade chicken overnight
2. Place chicken on the rack of a broiler pan and broil for 18-20 minutes
3. When ready, serve with lemon or grapes

Serves: *1*
Prep Time: 5   Minutes

Cook Time: 5   Minutes

Total Time: *10*   Minutes

INGREDIENTS

- 2 lettuce leaves
- ¾ oz. turkey breast
- 1 tablespoon mayonnaise
- 2 whole crackers
- 5-pieces grapes

DIRECTIONS

1. Cut turkey into small pieces
2. Top lettuce leaves with mayonnaise and turkey
3. Roll lettuce leaves and serve with crackers and grapes

Serves: **6**

Prep Time: **10**   Minutes

Cook Time: **15**   Minutes

Total Time: **25**   Minutes

INGREDIENTS

- ½ cup butter
- 1 tsp thyme
- zest of one orange
- 1 tsp minced garlic
- 2 lbs. shrimp
- ¼ tsp chili powder
- salt

DIRECTIONS

1. In a skillet add thyme leaves and simmer on low heat
2. Remove and add orange zest and cook for 2-3 minutes
3. Add garlic, shrimp, chili powder and cook for 4-5 minutes
4. When ready serve with pasta or rice

HONEY & GARLIC SHRIMP

Serves: **4**

Prep Time: **10** Minutes

Cook Time: **20** Minutes

Total Time: **30** Minutes

INGREDIENTS

- 1 tablespoon olive oil
- 1 tablespoon butter
- 1 lb. shrimp
- 2 garlic cloves
- 3 tablespoons honey
- 1 tablespoon soy sauce
- 2 tablespoons cilantro

DIRECTIONS

1. In a skillet add garlic, shrimp and cook for 5-6 minutes
2. In another bowl mix soy sauce, cilantro, honey, lime and mix well
3. Add the mixture to the skillet and bring to high heat
4. Cook for 4-5 minutes or until sauce reduces

Serves: **4**

Prep Time: **10**   Minutes

Cook Time: **30**   Minutes

Total Time: **40**   Minutes

INGREDIENTS

- 3 salmon steaks
- canola oil
- 1 tsp black pepper
- 1 cup arugula
- 1 tablespoon capers
- 2 slices lemon

DIRECTIONS

1. Brush salmon with canola oil
2. In a frying pan, fry salmon 3-4 minutes or until golden
3. Remove and serve with pepper and lemon

TOMATO AND BASIL SANDWICHES

Serves: **2**

Prep Time: **5**   Minutes

Cook Time: **5**   Minutes

Total Time: *10*   Minutes

INGREDIENTS

- 4 slices bread
- 6 tsp mayonnaise
- 2 slices tomato
- 2 tsp basil
- ¼ tsp salt
- ¼ tsp black pepper

DIRECTIONS

1. Spread mayonnaise over each bread slice
2. Top with basil, tomato slices, pepper, salt and top with bread
3. Serve when ready

OVEN-POACHED SALMON FILLETS

Serves: **2**

Prep Time: **10**   Minutes

Cook Time: **25**   Minutes

Total Time: **35**   Minutes

INGREDIENTS

- 1 lb. salmon fillet
- 1 tablespoon dry white wine
- ½ tsp salt
- ground black pepper
- 2 tablespoons shallot
- lemon wedges

DIRECTIONS

1. Preheat the oven to 400 F
2. In a pan place salmon with wine, shallots and pepper
3. Cover and bake for 20-25 minutes
4. When ready, remove and transfer to a plate
5. Serve with lemon wedges

OVEN FRIES

Serves: *2*

Prep Time: *10*   Minutes

Cook Time: *20*   Minutes

Total Time: *30*   Minutes

INGREDIENTS

- 1 gold potato
- 1 tsp olive oil
- ½ tsp salt
- ½ tsp dried thyme

DIRECTIONS

1. Preheat the oven to 425 F
2. Toss potato with salt, thyme and oil
3. Spread potato wedges on a baking sheet
4. Bake for 18-20 minutes or until tender
5. Remove and serve

LASAGNA ROLLS

Serves: **4**

Prep Time: **10** Minutes

Cook Time: **20** Minutes

Total Time: **30** Minutes

INGREDIENTS

- 10 lasagna noodles
- 1 tablespoon olive oil
- 2 cloves garlic
- 1 package tofu
- 2 cups spinach
- ¼ cup Parmesan cheese
- 2 tablespoons Kalamata olives
- ½ tsp red pepper
- ½ tsp salt
- 20 oz. marinara sauce
- ¼ cup mozzarella cheese

DIRECTIONS

1. In a pot add noodles, water and bring to a boil
2. In a skillet add garlic, tofu, spinach and cook for 4-5 minutes
3. Transfer to a bowl and stir in red pepper, marinara sauce, Parmesan and olives

4. Place a noodle on a cutting board and spread ¼ cup of the tofu filling

5. Roll up and place the roll in the pan, repeat with the remaining noodles

6. Bring to a simmer and reduce heat on medium for 5-6 minutes, remove when ready

7. Sprinkle with mozzarella and serve

LINGUINE WITH CLAMS

Serves: **4**

Prep Time: **10**   Minutes

Cook Time: **20**   Minutes

Total Time: **30**   Minutes

INGREDIENTS

- 8 oz. linguine pasta
- 1 tablespoon olive oil
- 1 clove garlic
- ½ tsp red pepper
- 28 oz. canned baby clams
- ½ cup dry white wine
- ½ cup chicken broth
- 2 tablespoons parsley

DIRECTIONS

1. Cook pasta according to package indications
2. In a skillet add garlic, red pepper and sauté for 2-3 minutes
3. Add reserved juice, broth, wine and bring to a boil for 5-6 minutes
4. Stir in clams, parsley and toss with pasta
5. Remove from heat and serve

OKRA FRITATTA

Serves: **2**

Prep Time: **10**   Minutes

Cook Time: **20**   Minutes

Total Time: **30**   Minutes

INGREDIENTS

- ½ lb. okra
- 1 tablespoon olive oil
- ½ red onion
- 2 eggs
- ¼ tsp salt
- 2 oz. cheddar cheese
- 1 garlic clove
- ¼ tsp dill

DIRECTIONS

1. In a bowl whisk eggs with salt and cheese
2. In a frying pan heat olive oil and pour egg mixture
3. Add remaining ingredients and mix well
4. Serve when ready

LEEK FRITATTA

Serves: **2**

Prep Time: **10**   Minutes

Cook Time: **20**   Minutes

Total Time: **30**   Minutes

INGREDIENTS

- ½ lb. leek
- 1 tablespoon olive oil
- ½ red onion
- ¼ tsp salt
- 2 ggs
- 2 oz. cheddar cheese
- 1 garlic clove
- ¼ tsp dill

DIRECTIONS

1. In a bowl whisk eggs with salt and cheese
2. In a frying pan heat olive oil and pour egg mixture
3. Add remaining ingredients and mix well
4. Serve when ready

KALE FRITATTA

Serves: **2**

Prep Time: **10**   Minutes

Cook Time: **20**   Minutes

Total Time: **30**   Minutes

INGREDIENTS

- 1 cup kale
- 1 tablespoon olive oil
- ½ red onion
- ¼ tsp salt
- 2 eggs
- 2 oz. cheddar cheese
- 1 garlic clove
- ¼ tsp dill

DIRECTIONS

1. In a skillet sauté kale until tender
2. In a bowl whisk eggs with salt and cheese
3. In a frying pan heat olive oil and pour egg mixture
4. Add remaining ingredients and mix well
5. Serve when ready

GREENS FRITATTA

Serves: **2**
Prep Time: **10**   Minutes

Cook Time: **20**   Minutes

Total Time: **30**   Minutes

INGREDIENTS

- ½ lb. greens
- 1 tablespoon olive oil
- ½ red onion
- ¼ tsp salt
- 2 eggs
- 2 oz. parmesan cheese
- 1 garlic clove
- ¼ tsp dill

DIRECTIONS

1. In a bowl whisk eggs with salt and parmesan cheese
2. In a frying pan heat olive oil and pour egg mixture
3. Add remaining ingredients and mix well
4. Serve when ready

BROCCOLI FRITATTA

Serves: **2**

Prep Time: **10** Minutes

Cook Time: **20** Minutes

Total Time: **30** Minutes

INGREDIENTS

- 1 cup broccoli
- 1 tablespoon olive oil
- ½ red onion
- ¼ tsp salt
- 2 oz. cheddar cheese
- 1 garlic clove
- ¼ tsp dill

DIRECTIONS

1. In a skillet sauté broccoli until tender
2. In a bowl whisk eggs with salt and cheese
3. In a frying pan heat olive oil and pour egg mixture
4. Add remaining ingredients and mix well
5. When ready serve with sautéed broccoli

PESTO PASTA WITH ASPARAGUS

Serves: **4**

Prep Time: **10**   Minutes

Cook Time: **20**   Minutes

Total Time: **30**   Minutes

INGREDIENTS

- 10 oz. shell pasta
- 1 lb. asparagus
- 2-3 tablespoons olive oil
- ¼ cup basil pesto
- ½ cup dried tomatoes
- ½ cup mozzarella cheese

DIRECTIONS

1. In a pot boil water and cook pasta
2. Place asparagus on a baking sheet drizzle olive oil and bake at 400 F for 12-15 minutes
3. In a bowl combine roasted asparagus, pasta, pesto and dried tomatoes
4. Top with mozzarella cheese and serve

RICE NOODLES

Serves: **2**

Prep Time: **10** Minutes

Cook Time: **20** Minutes

Total Time: **30** Minutes

INGREDIENTS

- 1 lb. rice noodles
- 2 tablespoons olive oil
- 1 red onion
- ½ lb. prawns
- 1 red pepper
- ¼ cucumber
- 1 tablespoon coriander leaves
- 3 tablespoon soy sauce
- 2 tablespoons fish sauce

DIRECTIONS

1. In a bowl combine soy sauce and fish sauce together
2. In a skillet heat olive oil and sauté onion until soft
3. Add prawns and sauce mixture to the skillet
4. Remove from heat, add pasta and remaining ingredients
5. Mix well and serve

EGG SANDWICH

Serves: **4**

Prep Time: **10** Minutes

Cook Time: **30** Minutes

Total Time: **40** Minutes

INGREDIENTS

- 1 lb. beetroot
- 2-3 bay leaves
- 2-3 eggs
- 2 tablespoons mayonnaise
- 2 celery sticks
- 1 pack mini peppers
- 1 gluten-free baton

DIRECTIONS

1. Slice the beetroot and fry for 2-3 minutes
2. Boil the eggs and cut in half
3. Cut the bread in half and spread mayonnaise on each bread half
4. Top with beetroot, bay leaves, celery sticks, peppers and boiled eggs
5. Serve when ready

CAULIFLOWER POPCORN

Serves: **4-6**

Prep Time: **10**   Minutes

Cook Time: **25**   Minutes

Total Time: **35**   Minutes

INGREDIENTS

- 1 cauliflower
- 1 tsp cumin
- 1 tsp turmeric
- 1 tsp chilies
- 1 tsp olive oil

DIRECTIONS

1. Cut the cauliflower into small pieces
2. In a bowl combine cumin, turmeric and chilies together
3. Add the cauliflower to the mixture and toss to coat
4. Drizzle olive oil and roast at 400 F for 22-25 minutes
5. When crispy remove from the oven and serve

ROASTED CAULIFLOWER WITH ORANGE DRESSING

Serves: *4*

Prep Time: *10*   Minutes

Cook Time: *30*   Minutes

Total Time: *40*   Minutes

INGREDIENTS

- 1 cauliflower
- 2 tablespoons olive oil
- 1 tsp cumin seeds
- 1 garlic clove
- 1 tsp chillies
- 1 tsp parsley
- Juice from 1 orange

DIRECTIONS

1. In a pan bring water to a boil and place the cauliflower
2. Simmer on medium heat for 5-10 minutes
3. In a bowl combine parsley, cumin seeds, chilies, olive oil and mix well
4. Toss the cauliflower florets with the mixture
5. Drizzle orange juice over the florets
6. Roast at 400 F for 18-20 minutes
7. When ready remove from the oven and serve

Serves:	*3-4*	
Prep Time:	*10*	Minutes
Cook Time:	*20*	Minutes
Total Time:	*30*	Minutes

INGREDIENTS

- 2 delicata squashes
- 2 tablespoons olive oil
- 1 tsp curry powder
- 1 tsp salt

DIRECTIONS

1. Preheat the oven to 400 F
2. Cut everything in half lengthwise
3. Toss everything with olive oil and place onto a prepared baking sheet
4. Roast for 18-20 minutes at 400 F or until golden brown
5. When ready remove from the oven and serve

Serves: **2**

Prep Time: **10**   Minutes

Cook Time: **20**   Minutes

Total Time: **30**   Minutes

INGREDIENTS

- 1 lb. brussels sprouts
- 1 tablespoon olive oil
- 1 tablespoon parmesan cheese
- 1 tsp garlic powder
- 1 tsp seasoning

DIRECTIONS

1. Preheat the oven to 425 F
2. In a bowl toss everything with olive oil and seasoning
3. Spread everything onto a prepared baking sheet
4. Bake for 8-10 minutes or until crisp
5. When ready remove from the oven and serve

PASTA

SIMPLE SPAGHETTI

Serves: 2

Prep Time: 5   Minutes

Cook Time: 15   Minutes

Total Time: 20   Minutes

INGREDIENTS

- 10 oz. spaghetti
- 2 eggs
- ½ cup parmesan cheese
- 1 tsp black pepper
- Olive oil
- 1 tsp parsley
- 2 cloves garlic

DIRECTIONS

1. In a pot boil spaghetti (or any other type of pasta), drain and set aside
2. In a bowl whish eggs with parmesan cheese
3. In a skillet heat olive oil, add garlic and cook for 1-2 minutes
4. Pour egg mixture and mix well
5. Add pasta and stir well

6. When ready garnish with parsley and serve

CORN PASTA

Serves: 2

Prep Time: 5   Minutes

Cook Time: 15   Minutes

Total Time: 20   Minutes

INGREDIENTS

- 1 lb. pasta
- 4 oz. cheese
- ¼ sour cream
- 1 onion
- 2 cloves garlic
- 1 tsp cumin
- 2 cups corn kernels
- 1 tsp chili powder
- 1 tablespoon cilantro

DIRECTIONS

1. In a pot boil spaghetti (or any other type of pasta), drain and set aside
2. Place all the ingredients for the sauce in a pot and bring to a simmer
3. Add pasta and mix well
4. When ready garnish with parmesan cheese and serve

ARTICHOKE PASTA

Serves: 2

Prep Time: 5   Minutes

Cook Time: 15   Minutes

Total Time: 20   Minutes

INGREDIENTS

- ¼ cup olive oil
- 1 jar artichokes
- 2 cloves garlic
- 1 tablespoon thyme leaves
- 1 lb. pasta
- 2 tablespoons butter
- 1. Cup basil
- ½ cup parmesan cheese

DIRECTIONS

1. In a pot boil spaghetti (or any other type of pasta), drain and set aside
2. Place all the ingredients for the sauce in a pot and bring to a simmer
3. Add pasta and mix well
4. When ready garnish with parmesan cheese and serve

CHICKEN PASTA

Serves: 2

Prep Time: 5   Minutes

Cook Time: 15   Minutes

Total Time: 20   Minutes

INGREDIENTS

- 1 lb. cooked chicken breast
- 8 oz. pasta
- 2 tablespoons butter
- 1 tablespoon garlic
- 1 tablespoon flour
- ½ cup milk
- ½ cup heavy cream
- 1 jar red bell peppers
- 2 tablespoons basil

DIRECTIONS

1. In a pot boil spaghetti (or any other type of pasta), drain and set aside
2. Place all the ingredients for the sauce in a pot and bring to a simmer
3. Add pasta and mix well
4. When ready garnish with parmesan cheese and serve

SHRIMP PASTA

Serves: 2

Prep Time: 5   Minutes

Cook Time: 15   Minutes

Total Time: 20   Minutes

INGREDIENTS

- ¼ cup mayonnaise
- ¼ cup sweet chili sauce
- 1 tablespoon lime juice
- 1 garlic clove
- 8 z. pasta
- 1 lb. shrimp
- ¼ tsp paprika

DIRECTIONS

1. In a pot boil spaghetti (or any other type of pasta), drain and set aside
2. Place all the ingredients for the sauce in a pot and bring to a simmer
3. Add pasta and mix well
4. When ready garnish with parmesan cheese and serve

PASTA WITH OLIVES AND TOMATOES

Serves: 2

Prep Time: 5   Minutes

Cook Time: 15   Minutes

Total Time: 20   Minutes

INGREDIENTS

- 8 oz. pasta
- 3 tablespoons olive oil
- 2 cloves garlic
- 5-6 anchovy fillets
- 2 cups tomatoes
- 1 cup olives
- ½ cup basil leaves

DIRECTIONS

1. In a pot boil spaghetti (or any other type of pasta), drain and set aside
2. Place all the ingredients for the sauce in a pot and bring to a simmer
3. Add pasta and mix well
4. When ready garnish with parmesan cheese and serve

SALAD

CHICKEN AND EGG SALAD

Serves: **2**

Prep Time: **5**   Minutes

Cook Time: **5**   Minutes

Total Time: **10**   Minutes

INGREDIENTS

- 2 chicken breasts
- 2 hard boiled eggs
- 2 tablespoons mayonnaise
- 1 tablespoon curry powder
- chives
- 1 pinch of salt

DIRECTIONS

1. In a bowl combine all ingredients together and mix well
2. Serve with dressing

TUNA NICOISE SALAD

Serves: **2**
Prep Time: **5**   Minutes

Cook Time: **5**   Minutes

Total Time: **10**   Minutes

INGREDIENTS

- 3 oz. tuna steak
- 1 egg
- 2 oz. spinach
- 2 oz. green beans
- 1 oz. broccoli
- ¼ red bell pepper
- 3 oz. cucumber
- 2 black olives
- 1 tsp olive oil
- 1 tsp balsamic vinegar

DIRECTIONS

1. In a bowl combine all ingredients together and mix well
2. Serve with dressing

TARRAGON CHICKEN SALAD

Serves: 2
Prep Time: 5 Minutes

Cook Time: 5 Minutes

Total Time: *10* Minutes

INGREDIENTS

- 1 lb. chicken breast
- 1 cup vegetable broth
- 1 bunch tarragon
- 1 lemon
- 2 black peppercorns
- 2 tablespoons sesame tahini
- 1 head lettuce
- 1 cup baby spinach leaves
- 1 orange
- ½ cup almonds

DIRECTIONS

1. In a bowl combine all ingredients together and mix well
2. Serve with dressing

Serves: **2**

Prep Time: 5   Minutes

Cook Time: 5   Minutes

Total Time: **10**   Minutes

INGREDIENTS

- 1 lb. watermelon
- 2 peaches
- 5 cups salad greens
- 1 cup feta cheese
- 1 tablespoon sunflower seeds

DIRECTIONS

1. **In a bowl combine all ingredients together and mix well**
2. **Serve with dressing**

CUCUMBER AND SCALLIONS SALAD

Serves: 2

Prep Time: 5   Minutes

Cook Time: 5   Minutes

Total Time: 10   Minutes

INGREDIENTS

- 3 pita breads
- 1 tablespoon olive oil
- 5 scallions
- ¾ tomatoes
- 1 cucumber
- 1 can tuna
- 1 tablespoon parsley
- 1 tablespoon cilantro
- 1 tablespoon mint
- salt

DIRECTIONS

1. In a bowl combine all ingredients together and mix well
2. Serve with dressing

SPINACH SALAD

Serves: **2**

Prep Time: **5** Minutes

Cook Time: **5** Minutes

Total Time: **10** Minutes

INGREDIENTS

- 2 oranges
- 1 grapefruit
- 5 cups baby spinach
- 3 scallions 3 oz. prosciutto

DRESSING

- 2 tablespoons balsamic vinegar
- 2 tablespoons olive oil
- 2 tablespoons cream
- 2 tsp honey
- ½ tsp salt
- ½ tsp black pepper

DIRECTIONS

1. In a bowl combine all ingredients together and mix well
2. Serve with dressing

SALMON SALAD

Serves: 2

Prep Time: 5   Minutes

Cook Time: 5   Minutes

Total Time: *10*   Minutes

INGREDIENTS

- 10 oz. grilled salmon
- 2 cups spinach
- 1 cup cucumber
- ¼ cup red onion

DRESSING

- 1 cup water
- 1 cup lemon juice
- 2 cup garlic cloves
- 2 tablespoons oregano
- 3 tablespoons flax seeds

DIRECTIONS

1. In a bowl combine all ingredients together and mix well
2. Serve with dressing

Serves: **2**

Prep Time: **5**   Minutes

Cook Time: **5**   Minutes

Total Time: **10** Minutes

INGREDIENTS

- 2 cups farro grain
- 2 tomatoes
- 1 cucumber
- ½ bunch parsley
- 3 cups greens
- 1 can chick peas

DRESSING

- ¼ cup tahini
- ¼ cup water
- ½ cup lemon juice
- 1 garlic clove
- ¼ tsp cumin

DIRECTIONS

1. **In a bowl combine all ingredients together and mix well**
2. **Serve with dressing**

THANK YOU FOR READING THIS BOOK!

CPSIA information can be obtained
at www.ICGtesting.com
Printed in the USA
BVHW071212180321
602885BV00007B/726

9 781664 024748